D1807658

JAPANESE FLAVOURS – MODERN CLASSICS

HIDEO DEKURA

PHOTOGRAPHY BY DANNY KILDARE

NH
NEW HOLLAND

First published in Australia in 2001 by
New Holland Publishers (Australia) Pty Ltd
Sydney • Auckland • London • Cape Town
14 Aquatic Drive Frenchs Forest NSW 2086 Australia
218 Lake Road Northcote Auckland New Zealand
86 Edgware Road London W2 2EA United Kingdom
80 McKenzie Street Cape Town 8001 South Africa

Copyright text © Hideo Dekura 2001
Copyright photography © Danny Kildare 2001
Copyright © New Holland Publishers (Aust.) Pty Ltd 2001

All rights reserved. No part of this publication may be
reproduced, stored in a retrieval system or transmitted,
in any form or by any means, electronic, mechanical,
photocopying, recording or otherwise, without the prior
written permission of the publishers and copyright holders.

National Library of Australia
Cataloguing-in-Publication Data:

Dekura, Hideo.
Japanese flavours: modern classics.

Includes index.
ISBN 1 86436 703 2.
1. Cookery, Japanese. I. Title.

641.5952

Publishing Manager: Anouska Good
Commissioned by: Averill Chase
Project Editor: Jennifer Lane
Designer: Nanette Backhouse
Photographer: Danny Kildare
Food Stylist: Keiko Yoshida
Kitchen Assistant: Noriko Kabuki
Production: Wendy Hunt
Reproduction: Colour Scan
Printer: Tat Wei Printing
Accessories kindly provided by Made in Japan,
Eastern Flair, David Hilsop Kiln Fired Glass,
Reject Shop, Wheel and Barrow and
the Tasmanian department
of Primary Industry.

Image page 16, a sake bottle; page 24, bamboo and
small dish; page 38, katsuo-bushi (dried bonito flakes);
page 46, quality lobster; page 56, vegetable cutters;
page 64, grilled and salted skewered sardines;
page 74, kanten (agar-agar) stick; page 82, tempura
pot with saibashi (cooking chopsticks); page 90,
wasabi plant; page 102, nanohana (canola);
page 114, Packham pear, nashi and Beurre Bosc
pear; page 124, Japanese teapot (kyūsu) and tea
cups (yunomi); page 128, Japanese sashimi slicing
knife (yanagiba-bōchō); page 142, bonsai.

DEDICATION

For my late brother Kenhyō Dekura (1936–1999), who devoted his life
to classical Japanese cuisine.

ACKNOWLEDGEMENTS

I am always enthusiastic to talk about classical Japanese cuisine with the
people around me. Thanks to all those who have shown interest in my
work and have helped me complete this book, especially New Holland
Publishers; Jennifer Lane, a great editor who understands Japanese food
and its cultural background; Danny Kildare, a great photographer and also
my personal friend; Nanette Backhouse, whose dramatic design is more
than I ever hoped for; Keiko Yoshida, who always encourages me and gives
a pep talk; and Gotaro Dekura, my son.

PREFACE

It is not easy to define what Japanese cuisine is in a few words. While *sushi*, *sashimi* and *tempura* are now quite commonplace dishes in some countries, they are only a few of the types of dishes within Japanese cuisine.

In Japan, the cuisine is divided into many categories according to the region, occasion and cooking style. In accordance with a strict, time-honoured tradition, professional Japanese cooking is taught by only the most highly respected headmasters and restaurant chefs. Their revered knowledge is passed on to their followers, who are rigorously trained in all aspects of Japanese food traditions, including floral arrangement and calligraphy, for traditionally, each guest is presented with a handwritten menu.

Moreover, Japanese food seems to vary depending on the consumers' age group and their accompanying tastes. Japanese youth tend to enjoy a wider variety of dishes, from supermarket food to ethnic food, and are quite comfortable with new styles of food and cooking. Older people, on the other hand, generally believe that their traditional eating habits are the secret of longevity, and they enjoy dishes such as cooked rice, vegetables, seafood and seaweed.

I learned traditional Japanese cooking styles and customs from my late father, Yutarō Dekura, my late brother, Kenhyō Dekura, and my mentor, Mr Shishikura, the founder of Shijyō-shinryu, an esteemed, traditional cooking school. All three were great chefs who influenced my cooking career enormously. While my father taught me home-style cooking according to our family traditions, Mr Shishikura taught me ceremonial Japanese cooking, which is founded on the beliefs of *Shintōism* (a native Japanese religion of nature and ancestor worship).

In this book, I introduce the traditional techniques, styles, ingredients and utensils used in Japanese cooking. The utensils and kitchenware I use are not only Japanese but also Western, so you do not need to rush out and buy a whole new set of dishes. The recipes cover entrées to desserts and the many Japanese courses in between, and have been designed to combine modern and traditional Japanese ingredients and methods. I encourage you to try them and to adapt them to your own needs.

In the beginning you may not be familiar with all the Japanese ingredients in the recipes. Rest assured that all of them are readily available from Japanese grocery shops and most can be found in some Asian (Chinese or Korean) grocery shops too. These days Japanese ingredients such as *nori* and *wasabi* are available even from local supermarkets.

Whether you're a novice or a professional cook, I hope that you enjoy this book and that it leads you to a growing interest in Japanese food.

HIDEO DEKURA

CONTENTS

INTRODUCTION

THE HISTORY OF JAPANESE FOOD

The close relationship between the Japanese people and rice has been interwoven with Japanese culture over the passage of time. Introduced from China and Korea at the beginning of Japanese history more than 2000 years ago, rice soon became such an important part of Japanese life that many ceremonies are associated with its growth cycle.

Japanese cuisine had its earliest roots in the beliefs of *Shintōism*, which greatly influenced the styles and motifs used in food, which was often part of the offering ceremonies to the Shintō gods. Korean and Chinese styles of vegetarian cuisine were then introduced, along with Buddhism, around the 8th century, and these were readily absorbed into Japanese culture and beliefs.

During the Heian era (794–1185AD), Japanese culture continued to flourish and absorb ideas from other Asian continents. Food preparation and cooking techniques were developed further in this period, including more sophisticated methods of steaming, stewing, pickling and grilling. Using these techniques, the Japanese people created the distinctive manner and fundamental styles of Japanese food that we know today, such as soup, stocks, pickles, sushi and sashimi. The *Zen* philosophy of Buddhism exerted a great influence on Japanese culture, teaching the theory of '*wabi*' (quiet refinement) and '*sabi*' (elegant simplicity); concepts which are still being developed in Japanese cuisine. The *Zen* influence is apparent in what is considered the proper way to handle ingredients, present Japanese dishes, and entertain guests.

Formal, ceremonial meals developed soon after the conclusion of the civil war era (1192–1333AD). *Honzen-ryōri*, one of the most formal full-course Japanese meals, introduced the practice of serving one soup and three dishes on a miniature table, using gorgeous lacquerware and crockery. (The miniature table has evolved into a tray at many restaurants today.) This led to the development of *chakaiseki-ryōri* (*kaiseki*), a full course meal and tea ceremony, and *kaiseki-ryōri*, a full course banquet.

The first official cooking groups and schools were founded around 1300AD. These schools have upheld traditions and passed them down through many generations. Through these schools Japanese culinary skills have been maintained in all their beauty and tradition for more than 700 years.

In the Edo era (1600–1867AD) the government cut off their relationships with other countries and a national isolation policy was enacted. Under these circumstances, Japanese culture found its own way, producing developments in the tea ceremony, food culture, and most of the Japanese arts without influences from any other countries. When the isolation policy ended, the people were so excited to meet the unknown western culture that the society underwent a remarkable change in its culture and traditions. Many foods were introduced from Europe, such as bread, coffee, confectioneries, whisky, and wine. Moreover, the habit of eating meat became widely accepted among the people of Japan.

However, the last decade has seen a striking revival of Japanese traditions, including food culture, in Japan. The number of restaurants and food industries in Japan reached a peak just before the year 2000. Throughout the history of Japanese food, changes in society and influences from overseas have had marked effects. Without these, Japanese food could not have developed into the wonderful cuisine that we know today.

JAPANESE FOOD TODAY

In every culture, eating and drinking together play a significant role in creating and maintaining relationships. Japanese meals vary according to the needs of the occasion. The main styles are the family meal, the packed meal and the formal meal. There are four fundamental types of traditional full-course Japanese formal meals today: *honzen-ryōri*, an assembly of dishes served on a tray at formal banquets; *chakaiseki-ryōri*, a series of dishes served before the tea ceremony; *kaiseki-ryōri*, a series of dishes for parties, often served at restaurants specialising in Japanese cuisine (*ryōtei*); and *shōjin-ryōri*, Buddhist vegetarian dishes.

The art of Japanese food arrangement is characterised by certain broad concepts. Foremost among these is the concept that empty space has a beauty of its own. The balance between vessel and space, and space and food, are also considered crucial. This balance varies according to the season, the design of the utensils and tableware, the type of food, the venue, and even the age of the guests. When multicoloured foods are arranged on serving dishes, great attention is paid to spacing—where and how to leave empty areas to best emphasise the beauty of the dish. This is based on the concept of *ma*: space as a dynamic entity, and an integral and vital component of any composition. The beauty of a finished dish is considered as important as the various ingredients that go into its composition.

Traditionally, the Japanese take their meals seated on *tatami* floor matting, with a small tray-table for each diner. This is still common at traditional Japanese restaurants or inn-style hotels. In Japan, individual servings are laid out on each tray-table beforehand, and carried to the diners. Timing is essential: one must be alert to the guests' state of mind and offer the meal at the proper juncture. The menu may be written in one of three styles of calligraphy: *shin, gyō* and *sō. Shin* (plain, true) is a clear, basic style; *gyō* (running) is a more cursive style; and *sō* (grass) is a still more cursive form. The style of the calligraphy on the menu is a clear indication of the style of food presentation the diner can expect of that dish.

The Japanese have an overwhelming predilection for odd numbers, based on the ancient philosophy of yin and yang and the five elements. According to this philosophy, even numbers are *yin* (negative), and odd ones are *yang* (positive). This belief is reflected in Japanese cooking to this day; witness *sashimi*, which is usually presented in groups of three, five or seven slices.

It is impossible to discuss Japanese culture without reference to nature. Japan's climate is characterised by pronounced seasonal changes, and the rhythms of life inevitably follow the shifting seasons. The Japanese are very observant of the changes of season, and prepare dishes to reflect these changes. This sensitivity to the seasons is at its strongest in the tea ceremony. In *kaiseki-ryōri*, select foods are served on individual trays as part of the tea ceremony, with a special emphasis placed on the three *ki: kisetsu* (season), *ki* (vessel) and *kikai* (occasion). Each occasion is considered unique, and hospitality is heightened by serving fresh food, in season, to bring out the flavour, aroma and colour of the ingredients.

According to an old proverb, eating the first produce of the season adds seventy-five days to one's life, so Japanese people always look forward to welcoming a new season. Four seasonal recipes are featured on the following pages, each celebrating the bounty one of the seasons.

GRILLED SNAPPER COVERED WITH SALT

You will need 2 steel BBQ skewers for
each snapper

SERVES 4

4 whole small snapper, 300g (10oz) each
1 tablespoon mirin
½ cup (125g/4oz) ground rock salt
4 lemon wedges
soy sauce
8 red radishes, thinly sliced

Spring is the season in which every creature starts to wake up after winter.
The wealth of marine and farm products in this season is a delight, and a
plate of sushi can reflect the sudden joy of nature blossoming in the gardens.
Pink cherry blossom is the most loved spring flower in Japan, and this colour
often extends to spring dishes. Here it is seen in the colour of the baby
snapper and radishes.

Preheat the oven to 180°C (350°F).

Scale the snappers and make a shallow slit along the belly side of each fish.
Remove and discard the insides, washing well under running water. Wipe
dry thoroughly with paper towels. Place a fish on its side on a cutting board.
Push a skewer all the way through the tail just above the line of the backbone.
Without removing the skewer, push it back through the fish at a point near
the top edge of the fish, level with the gills. The skewer should run along
the outside of the fish, thus creating a slight curve through its body. Push
another skewer through the tail just below the line of the backbone.
Without removing the skewer, push it back through the fish at a point near
the belly edge of the fish, just behind the gills. Repeat for each fish. Sprinkle
over the *mirin* and rock salt.

Place the fish on a lightly oiled baking tray in the middle of the oven. Cook
for 10 minutes with the door kept open to ensure good air circulation. This
will give the flesh a slightly drier texture and a more intense flavour. Preheat
the grill to medium heat. Transfer to the grill and cook until the skin becomes
a nice brown colour. Test to see if the fish is cooked through by inserting a
bamboo skewer near the bone. If juice appears on the surface, keep cooking.

To serve, remove the skewers, arrange the fish on serving plates and garnish
each with a lemon wedge. Arrange sliced red radish over one side of each fish.
Offer soy sauce on the side for dipping.

SPRING SUSHI

This recipe is pictured together with pieces of Kakumaki (Square Nori Roll) *sushi*.
If you wish to include it in your spring dish, follow the recipe on page 97)

SUMMER

夏

GREEN TEA SOBA AND SŌMEN NOODLES

SERVES 4

4 litres (8 pints) water
120g (4oz) sōmen, *divided into four equal bunches*
120g (4oz) green tea soba, *divided into four equal bunches*
ice cubes
12 pieces canned mandarine
2 spring onion (scallions) stems, chopped, or 4 Japanese basil flowers
shichimi *(Japanese seven-spice powder) and* wasabi *to serve*

DIPPING SAUCE
½ cup (125ml/4fl oz) Bonito Dashi *(see page 144)*
½ cup (125ml/4fl oz) soy sauce
½ cup (125ml/4fl oz) mirin

Cold drinks and light dishes are appropriate for a hot summer's day. A bowl of chilled noodles, sashimi on a bed of ice, and fresh salads are cooling and provide stamina.

Bring 2 litres (4 pints) of water to the boil in a large saucepan. Tie one end of each bunch of *sōmen* with a rubber band. Put the *sōmen* in the boiling water and cook for 2–3 minutes until al dente. Drain, then rinse the *sōmen* thoroughly under running water to remove the starch. Drain well again.

Bring another 2 litres (4 pints) of water to the boil. Divide the *soba* into 2 bundles, and tie one end of each with a rubber band. Put the *soba* in the boiling water and cook until al dente, or according to the directions on the packet. Drain, then rinse the *soba* thoroughly. Drain well again.

Place the ice cubes in 4 deep serving bowls. Place 2 bamboo sticks across the top of each bowl. Cut off the tied ends of the *sōmen* and *soba* and hang the noodles on the bamboo sticks. Arrange the mandarines on the ice.

To make the dipping sauce, combine all the ingredients in a bowl. Divide the sauce among the 4 serving bowls. Place the spring onion or basil flowers, *shichimi* and *wasabi* on a plate where diners can help themselves.

To eat, place the spring onions, *shichimi* and *wasabi* in the dipping sauce. Dip the noodles into the sauce before eating.

FUKI-YOSE OF AUTUMN VEGETABLES

SERVES 4

4 chestnuts
8 ginkgo nuts
1 cup (250g/80oz) rock salt
2 tablespoons olive oil
8 shimeji mushrooms
8 nameko *mushrooms (*enoki *may be substituted*
if nameko *are not available)*
4 fresh shitake *mushrooms*
12 momiji (maple-leaf) shaped carrots
(see page 151)
2 tablespoons sake *(Japanese rice wine)*
8 dried yuzu pieces
80g (2¾oz) daikon, grated
4 chives, finely chopped

SAUCE
¼ cup (60ml/2fl oz) Bonito Dashi
(see page 144)
¼ cup (60ml/2fl oz) soy sauce
¼ cup (60ml/2fl oz) mirin

The vegetables in this dish are cooked on heated stones. You will need about 2 cups of medium-sized stones and some wire mesh to place them on for cooking. A cake-cooling rack may suffice. Yuzu-miso *can be used in place of the sauce.*

Preheat the oven to 180°C (350°F).

To prepare the chestnuts and ginkgo nuts, make a tiny slit in each shell. Place the chestnuts and ginkgo nuts in 2 separate pots of water and bring the water to the boil in both. The ginkgo nuts will need 10 minutes over medium heat and the chestnuts 15 minutes. Drain the nuts when they are done.

Place a wire mesh over an element on the stove top, add the stones and heat. Alternatively, place the stones beneath an oven grill. The stones are hot enough when a few drops of water placed on them fizz and evaporate instantly. Spread the rock salt in a medium-sized gratin dish or a clay cooking pot, and place the dish in the oven for 10 minutes.

Take the dish out of the oven, and place it on a pot stand. With tongs, place the heated stones on the dish. Sprinkle with olive oil. Arrange the chestnuts, nuts, *shimeji*, *nameko* and *shitake* mushrooms and carrots on the stones, and sprinkle with sake. Cover with aluminium foil or a lid, and set aside outside the oven for about 15 minutes to steam.

To make the sauce, combine the *dashi*, soy sauce and *mirin* in a pan. Simmer gently for 5 minutes. Pour the sauce into 4 dipping bowls and divide the *yuzu* among the bowls.

Transfer the dish with the vegetables to the table and remove the foil or lid. Serve with grated *daikon*, chopped chives, and sauce on the side.

WINTER

冬

Beef Mizutaki Hot Pot

SERVES 4

4 *dried* shītake *mushrooms*
80g (2¾oz) harusame *(Japanese vermicelli)*
100g (3½oz) momen-dōfu
(firm beancurd), quartered
40g (1½oz) takenoko *(bamboo shoots), diced*
4 *strips* kombu *(kelp), each*
1cm (⅜in)x 4cm (1½in), knotted
400g (14oz) beef, thinly sliced
8 shungiku *(spring chrysanthemum) leaves*
12 shimeji *mushrooms*
6 *cups (1.5 litres/3 pints) Bonito Dashi*
(see page 144)

DIPPING SAUCE
2 *tablespoons white sesame paste (tahini)*
4 *tablespoons castor sugar*
4 *teaspoons* mirin
4 *teaspoons soy sauce*
4 *tablespoons rice vinegar*

ACCOMPANIMENTS
80g (2¾oz) daikon, *grated*
4 *chives, finely chopped*
shichimi *(Japanese seven-spice powder)*

On a cold winter's day, a dish rich in protein, served steaming hot, brings a precious feeling to the body and soul. Dishes are cooked for longer, sake is served hot, and even fish have a higher fat content and a richer taste. In Japanese cuisine, there are several styles of pot dishes, including sukiyaki, shabu-shabu and mizutaki. Sukiyaki is prepared in a special iron pan at the table by cooking thinly sliced beef together with various vegetables, beancurd and harusame (Japanese vermicelli). Shabu-shabu is prepared in a special copper pan by cooking thinly sliced beef and various vegetables in boiling water. It is served with a special white sesame sauce. Mizutaki literally means 'water-simmered cooking'.

Hot pot dishes are traditionally cooked at the table using a portable gas cooker or hibachi. An earthenware claypot is used for this dish to keep it warm. There are various sizes of pots available, from small dishes for 1–2 people to large dishes for up to 8 people.

Reconstitute the dried *shītake* mushrooms by soaking them in some warm water for about 30 minutes or until the caps are soft. Cut and discard the stems and reserve the caps.

Bring a pot of water to the boil and add the *harusame*. Cook for 1 minute, then drain well and set aside.

To make the dipping sauce, whisk the sesame paste, sugar, *mirin*, soy sauce and rice vinegar in a bowl until well combined. Divide sauce among 4 bowls.

Arrange the *momen-dōfu, harusame, shītake* mushrooms, *takenoko, kombu,* beef and *shungiku* in 4 small, heatproof ceramic pots. Pour the *dashi* into the 4 pots. Place each pot on a *hibachi* or portable stove, and bring to the boil.

Serve and eat over heat with dipping sauce and accompaniments on the side.

創作日本料理

五神　大吟醸

芳醇馥郁
入魂一滴
典雅繊細

奈良県五條市今井一丁目二一三

五條酒造

清

SHOKU-ZEN SHU (APÉRITIFS)

Alcoholic drinks are sometimes served as an apéritif before a meal to stimulate the appetite. Rather than the Scotch, cognac or champagne-based drinks that often precede a western-style meal, fruity alcoholic drinks such as plum, orange or mandarine in *sake* are served before a Japanese meal. The traditional, fruity style of these drinks complements Japanese food well, however Japanese drinks are gradually beginning to incorporate more new ingredients from other Asian and western countries too.

19 MATCHA AND LEMONGRASS COCKTAIL
     抹茶とレモングラスのカクテル

19 STRAWBERRY CHAMPAGNE COCKTAIL
     イチゴのシャンペン・カクテル

21 APRICOT SAKE
     杏子酒

21 GRAPEFRUIT AND MANDARINE SAKE
     グレープフルーツと蜜柑酒

22 SAKE, HOT SAKE, COLD SAKE
     酒

MATCHA AND LEMONGRASS COCKTAIL
抹茶とレモングラスのカクテル

SERVES 4

4 teaspoons matcha *(green tea) powder*
250 ml (8fl oz) Midori
12 ice cubes
1 stem lemongrass, 10cm (4in) long

Midori *is a Japanese liqueur with the flavour of green honeydew melon. You can purchase it from any liquor shop.*

With a small whisk, mix the *matcha* powder and 1 tablespoon *Midori* in a small bowl until the *matcha* dissolves.

Pour the mixture into a cocktail shaker, add the remaining *Midori* and ice cubes, and shake. Strain into 4 cocktail glasses.

Cut the lemongrass lengthwise into 4 pieces and use to garnish the cocktail (as pictured).

STRAWBERRY CHAMPAGNE COCKTAIL
イチゴのシャンペン・カクテル

SERVES 4

8 strawberries, hulled
60ml (2fl oz) sweet sherry
250ml (8fl oz) champagne, chilled

Purée the strawberries in a blender until smooth. Pass the purée through a strainer.

Shake the strawberry purée and sweet sherry in a cocktail shaker. Pour into champagne glasses, and pour over the chilled champagne.

APRICOT SAKE

MAKES 380ml (13fl oz)

180g (6oz) dried apricot halves
70g (2½oz) castor sugar
210ml (7fl oz) sake (Japanese rice wine)
mint leaves, for garnish

Apricot sake *takes six to twelve months to mature.*

Combine the dried apricots, sugar and *sake* in an airtight container and refrigerate. Every three months, shake lightly with lid on.

After six months, the apricots will change colour to a golden brown. You can start drinking the *sake* from this time. If you leave it for another six months, the flavour will gain more maturity.

To serve, chill and strain the apricot *sake* into glasses, and garnish with mint leaves (as pictured opposite at left).

GRAPEFRUIT AND MANDARINE SAKE

MAKES 380ml (13fl oz)

210ml (7fl oz) sake (Japanese rice wine)
zest of 2 large mandarines
zest of 1 large grapefruit
70g (2½oz) crystal sugar, crushed
½ teaspoon mandarine zest (extra) or
grapefruit zest (extra)

Citrus sake *takes three to six months to mature.*

Pour the *sake* into an airtight container, add the citrus zest and crystal sugar. Refrigerate for three to six months. The *sake* improves with time.

To serve, strain the *sake* and serve in a glass with fresh zest (as pictured opposite at right).

SAKE

酒

Sake is a Japanese alcoholic drink based on three ingredients: rice, yeast and water. Since early times (c. 700AD) sake and Shintōism have been closely entwined. Even today, each new vintage of sake is presented to the gods in elaborately decorated barrels to thank them for the year's abundant harvest.

Sake is produced in many places throughout Japan. The different qualities of rice and water in each region contribute to the unique taste of each manufacturer's sake. Along with these differences, there are also many variations due to different methods of production. Sake ranges from dry to fairly sweet. Dry sake is called kara-kuchi and sweet is ama-kuchi.

The four main varieties of sake are Junmai-shu, Ginjyō-shu, Honjyōzō-shu and Kizake. Junmai-shu is made in the most traditional manner, from rice, water and yeast only. It is quite rich and has a dominant rice flavour. Ginjyō-shu is considered the ultimate sake, though it is expensive and hard to find, as it is made in very limited quantities. Ginjyō-shu has a sweet taste and a fruity aroma, and is best served cold or slightly warm. Honjyōzō-shu is a mild-flavoured sake with added alcohol which must not exceed 25 per cent of the total alcohol content.

Sake is traditionally served with a meal or food of some kind. Salty food is considered a good companion for sake. Tsumami (a selection of savoury morsels), is a common accompaniment to pre-dinner drinks. If taken with a meal, the choice of a sweet or dry variety would depend on the individual's taste, rather than any gastronomic prerequisite. These days, fruity sake cocktails have become very popular in izakaya (pubs) in Japan.

Cold sake is popular in summer or when served as an apéritif. Warm sake is popular in winter, but is enjoyed at any time of the year with a meal. Warming the sake reduces the alcohol content but enhances the aroma and flavour.

HOT SAKE

Although Japanese people commonly refer to warm *sake* as 'hot *sake*', it is never heated over 50°C (200°F). To prepare hot *sake*, pour *sake* into a *tokkuri* (a small sake serving bottle). Bring a pot of water to the boil and place the *tokkuri* in the water. Heat until the *sake* reaches 35°–50°C (100°–200°F). Using a cloth, remove the *tokkuri* from the pot and wipe away any excess water. Serve warm in small *sake* cups (*ochoko*).

COLD SAKE

Cold *sake* can be kept at room temperature. It does not need to be chilled in the refrigerator. In summer, cold *sake* served straight in a small cup or a small liqueur glass is a refreshing drink.

ENTRÉES

Whether you're planning an elaborate drinks party or inviting a few friends for dinner, starters should be light, but appeal to the eye. Think about your guests, their particular tastes and the occasion. Is it a 'spring party', a 'celebration party' or just a 'long-time-no-see' party? The food should help set the mood.

Devote your time to making a prelude that gives guests a nice expectation of the main dishes. The flavours, textures and colours of the foods should complement each other as well as the course that follows.

For inspiration, find out what's in season and plentiful at the markets. It is always best to use ingredients at their peak.

STEAMED SEA URCHIN WITH SAKE

うにの酒蒸し

Kinome, *the young leaves of the prickly ash* (sanshō) *tree, is available from Japanese grocery stores in spring. The leaves have a highly aromatic flavour and are a popular garnish.*

Fresh takenoko *(bamboo shoot) is available from some Asian and Japanese grocery stores in spring, and pre-cooked fresh* takenoko *is sold in vacuum packs. Chinese bamboo shoots with seasonings are not suitable for Japanese cooking, so check this before you buy. Frozen Chinese bamboo shoots without seasoning can be substituted.*

Reconstitute the dried *shītake* mushrooms by soaking in some warm water until the caps are soft. Cut off and discard the stems and reserve the caps.

SERVES 4

4 *dried* shītake *mushrooms*
4 *fresh whole sea urchins in the shell*
100g *(3½ oz)* takenoko *(bamboo shoots)*
4 *tablespoons* sake *(Japanese rice wine)*
4 *sprigs* kinome *(young sanshō leaves)*

DIPPING SAUCE
1 *tablespoon* mirin
4 *tablespoons soy sauce*

To open the sea urchins, insert the point of a knife into their undersides (where there are no spikes) and prise open. Try to minimise damage to the shells, as you will need them to present the dish. Use your fingers to gently remove the yellow roe. Set aside. Rinse the shells under running water.

Peel the *takenoko* and cook in boiling water until tender. Drain and slice. Divide the sliced *takenoko* and mushrooms among the upturned sea urchin shells and sprinkle with *sake*. Top with the sea urchin roe.

Bring water to the boil in a steamer, and carefully place the filled shells inside. Steam for about 20 minutes over medium heat. (If you have purchased sea urchins without shells, steam the roe in teacups covered with foil, steam the *takenoko* and mushrooms in a regular steamer, and assemble on separate plates to serve.)

When ready, transfer the shells to serving plates. Garnish each with a *kinome* sprig.

Combine the *mirin* and soy sauce in a separate dish and serve on the side as a dipping sauce.

LOTUS ROOT AND TOMATOES WITH SANSHŌ VINAIGRETTE

蓮根とトマトの酢のもの

Fresh lotus root is available from Asian grocery shops during winter. Frozen sliced lotus root can be substituted through the year. Sanshō (Japanese mountain pepper) is different from Western pepper: while peppery, it also has a grassy aroma. Ground sanshō is more readily available than seeds and may be used instead. Lemon grass can be used in place of the sanshō—the effect is quite different, however.

SERVES 4

4 kombu *(kelp) strips*
200g (7oz) renkon *(fresh lotus root), peeled and thinly sliced*
20 cherry tomatoes
12 miner's lettuce (winter purslane) or butter lettuce leaves

SANSHŌ VINAIGRETTE
1 teaspoon sanshō
1 tablespoon mirin
1 cup (250ml/8fl oz) rice vinegar
⅓ cup (80ml/3fl oz) water
⅓ cup (80g/3oz) castor sugar

To make the *sanshō* vinaigrette, combine all the ingredients and mix well, stirring until the sugar dissolves. Set aside.

Cook the *kombu* strips in boiling water for 5 minutes. Remove from water and set aside.

Cook the *renkon* in boiling water for 2 minutes. Drain.

Blanch the tomatoes in boiling water for 10–20 seconds, then plunge them into iced water. Remove 4 tomatoes and set aside. Remove and peel remaining tomatoes, discarding the skins. Score the skin of each unpeeled tomato into quarters from the bottom. Take care not to cut the flesh. Peel the four scored 'flaps' back towards the top of the tomato, but leave each flap attached at the top. Gather the four flaps together and tie them up neatly with a *kombu* strip.

Marinate the *renkon* and all the tomatoes in the vinaigrette and refrigerate for 40 minutes.

To serve, arrange lettuce leaves or snowpea sprouts on the base of 4 serving plates. Arrange four tomatoes on top, and finish with a slice of *renkon*.

Top the *renkon* with a *kombu*-tied tomato, pour over the *sanshō* vinaigrette and serve chilled.

CHEDDAR CHEESE WITH UME PASTE AND NORI

チーズと海苔の重ね焼き

If shiso-ume *paste is not available, you could use* ume-boshi *(pickled plum) purée instead. Other suitable alternatives include roasted black sesame mixed with grated ginger, or white* miso *combined with* mirin, *or simply a sprinkle of* yuzu *powder.*

Preheat the oven to 180°C (350°F).

Place a *nori* square on a dry board. Arrange a cheddar slice on the *nori* sheet. With a butter knife, spread 2 teaspoons of *shiso-ume* paste on top of the cheddar. Top with another *nori* sheet. Place another cheddar slice on the *nori* sheet, and spread with 2 teaspoons of *shiso-ume* paste.

Continue layering until the last slice of cheese has been used, then place the last *nori* sheet on top. With a knife, cut the stack into quarters.

Carefully lift each portion onto a baking sheet. Tie each stack with two chives, tucking the ends underneath. Place in the preheated oven and when the cheese starts melting (this should take no longer than 10 seconds), transfer to a serving plate.

Top each portion with an olive and serve.

SERVES 4

1 sheet nori, *cut to the same size as the cheese*
5 slices cheddar cheese (use ready-cut slices)
8 teaspoons shiso-ume *(Japanese plum and* shiso *paste)*
8 chives
4 stuffed green Spanish olives

KING PRAWN WRAPPED IN HARUSAME

Harusame *literally means 'spring rain'. When cooked,* harusame *noodles take on a transparency reminiscent of a light, springtime rain shower. In this recipe the colour of the prawn glows through the* harusame.

To make the *kimizu* mixture, combine the egg yolks, vinegar and *mirin* in a bowl and mix well. Set aside until ready to use.

Dip the *mitsuba* in boiling water until wilted. Drain then refresh in cold water for a few seconds. Drain and set aside.

SERVES 4
8 leaves mitsuba *(trefoil)*
8 king prawns (giant shrimp), shelled, with heads and tails left on
150g (5 oz) ugo
100g (3½oz) harusame *(Japanese vermicelli)*
8 chives (at least 10cm/4in lengths)

KIMIZU MIXTURE
2 egg yolks
1 tablespoon rice vinegar
1 tablespoon mirin

Thread each prawn onto a bamboo skewer to straighten it. Blanch the prawns in boiling water until the shells turn a nice reddish colour. Remove the prawns from the heat and refresh in cold water for a couple of minutes. Drain well. Remove prawn heads but do not discard them.

Rinse ugo under cold running water. Drain and set aside.

Cut the *harusame* so that they are slightly shorter than the prawns. Cook the *harusame* in boiling water over medium heat, stirring occasionally with chopsticks or a fork until transparent. Drain, then chill under running water. Drain well. Lay a band of *harusame* 5cm (2in) wide on a board (this should use one-eighth of the *harusame*). Place a prawn lengthways on the *harusame*. Gather the *harusame* around the prawn and tie at both ends with chives. Repeat with the other prawns and remaining *harusame*.

Clean out and rinse the prawn heads. Dry them thoroughly with paper towels. Place a handful of ugo in each bowl and top with 2 prawns wrapped in *harusame* and 2 prawn heads. Insert a small piece of *mitsuba* into each *harusame* package.

Serve with the *kimizu* mixture.

TŌFU WITH YUZU MISO

焼き豆腐

Momen-dōfu *has a firmer texture than other varieties of* tōfu, *making it ideal for stewing and grilling. It is available in packets in small blocks or as a whole block. Choose the one in small blocks for this recipe.* Yuzu miso *is made of* miso *and* yuzu *(Japanese citrus) zest. This soybean paste tastes sweet and is good for delicate dressings and sauces.*

SERVES 4

300g (10oz) momen-dōfu *(firm beancurd)*
iced water
8 English spinach leaves
8 sprigs kinome *(young* sanshō *leaves) or*
kaiware-daikon (daikon *sprout) or*
mustard cress

DIPPING SAUCE
¼ cup (60ml/2fl oz) yuzu miso*
1 tablespoon mirin

Cut the *tōfu* into 8 pieces about 5cm (2in) square. Bring some salted water to the boil in a pan and gently blanch the *tōfu*. Take the *tōfu* out of the pot and refresh in iced water. Drain well.

To make the dipping sauce, combine the *yuzu miso* and *mirin* in a small bowl and mix well.

Blanch the spinach leaves in some salted boiling water. Drain, then refresh in cold water. Drain again and squeeze out any excess water.

To serve, place a square of *tōfu* on each plate, followed by a thin layer of spinach. Place another piece of *tōfu* on top. Heat the tip end of a steel skewer until hot and scorch the top of the *tōfu* in a checked pattern.

Top each portion with 2 *kinome* sprigs. Spoon a little dipping sauce beside the *tōfu* and serve.

*You can replace *yuzu miso* with a mixture of 1 teaspoon of ground roasted black sesame seeds and ¼ cup (60ml/2fl oz) white *miso*, mixed using a *suribachi* or mortar and pestle.

JAPANESE-STYLE ESCABÈCHE OF SARDINES

SERVES 4

Anchovies or pilchards can be used for this recipe instead of sardines.

½ cup (125g/4oz) katakuriko *(potato starch) or cornstarch*
8 whole sardines
4 cups (1 litre/2 pints) vegetable oil, for deep-frying
1 onion, sliced
1 tablespoon roasted white sesame seeds
4 dried red chillies (whole)
4 pairs of pine needles or toothpicks, for skewers

To prepare the vinegar mixture, combine the sugar, rice vinegar and sesame oil in a bowl and whisk until well combined and the sugar is dissolved.

Coat the sardines in the *katakuriko* then place them aside on paper towels for about 5 minutes.

Heat the oil in a heavy-based pan or wok over a medium heat until it reaches 180°C (350°F). Test heat with a small piece of bread—when it crisps up and floats to the top, the oil is hot enough. Fry the sardines until golden brown. Drain on clean paper towels.

VINEGAR MIXTURE
¼ cup (60g/2oz) castor sugar
1 cup (250ml/8fl oz) rice vinegar
1 teaspoon sesame oil

Combine the sardines with the vinegar mixture. Add the sliced onion, sesame seeds and chillies. Chill for 30 minutes. Knot the ends of the pine needles and thread sardines together in pairs. Serve as pictured opposite, allowing two sardines per person.

DEEP-FRIED WHITING IN SHISO-UME

SERVES 4

Yukari, *Japanese 'red' basil (it is actually purple), is available from some Asian grocery and Japanese grocery stores. Allow around 90g (3oz) fish per person.*

4 whiting fillets (360g/12oz total weight), skin on
1 teaspoon sake
2 tablespoons katakuriko *(potato starch)*
200ml (7fl oz) vegetable oil, for deep-frying
100g (3½oz) shiso-ume *(Japanese plum and* shiso *paste)*
2 teaspoons yukari

Carefully check fillets and remove any bones with a pair of tweezers. Cut the fillets into bite-sized pieces, and sprinkle with sake.

Place the *katakuriko* on a tray, and coat the fish.

Heat the oil in a deep heavy-based pan or a wok and fry the fish until golden brown. Drain well on paper towels or a wire rack.

Place the *shiso-ume* in a bowl and add the fish, tossing lightly to coat. Arrange the fish on serving plates and sprinkle over the *yukari*. Serve hot.

SOUPS

Dairy products such as milk and cream are hardly ever used in traditional Japanese soups. Ingredients such as fish, prawns, *kombu* (kelp), *shitake* mushrooms and spring onions (scallions) are used to flavour soups instead. The inclusion of ingredients such as *tōfu* or elaborately carved vegetables gives the soup an identifiable Japanese signature. Unlike western soups, which are usually cooked for a long time, and with most ingredients combined, Japanese soups are cooked gently, and should not be boiled. Moreover, they are served as part of the main meal, not before it.

Soups are roughly divided into three groups: clear soup, *miso* soup and others (such as cold soup with sieved vegetables, and thicker soups with chicken or pork stock).

COLD GREEN PEA SOUP WITH DAIKON FLOWER

冷製グリーン・ピースと大根の花

This is an ideal summer soup.

Cut the *daikon* into 4 equal sections no thicker than 2.5cm (1in). Using a flower-shaped vegetable cutter, cut out a flower shape. (A round, square or star-shaped cutter can be used instead.)

SERVES 4

1 medium-sized daikon, peeled and cut into a long block
2 cups (500ml/16fl oz) hot water
2 chicken or vegetable bouillon stock cubes
2 tablespoons mirin
1 cup (150g/5oz) fresh or frozen green peas
½ cup (120ml/4fl oz) thick cream
1 quantity Egg Mimosa (see page 147)
1 teaspoon tobikko (flying fish roe)

Combine the hot water and bouillon cubes in a pan and stir with a spatula until the cubes dissolve. Add the *daikon* and simmer for 15 minutes or until soft. Turn off the heat, then chill the *daikon* and bouillon in the refrigerator.

Drizzle the *mirin* over the peas in a bowl and mix gently. Bring some water to the boil in a pan, add the peas and cook until they soften. Drain, then refresh the peas under running water. Transfer to a blender or a food processor and purée. Pass the purée through a sieve to get a smooth mixture.

Place the purée in a bowl and add the cream. Mix well with a spatula and refrigerate until chilled.

To serve, pour the soup into individual bowls. Place a *daikon* flower in the middle and top with some egg mimosa and a little *tobikko*.

GREEN WINTER MELON WITH FISH CAKE IN CLEAR SOUP

冬瓜とすり身のお吸いもの

Green winter melon belongs to the marrow vegetable group, and is not a 'melon' as such. It has a fat, long shape with white flesh surrounded by green skin. Fish paste is available frozen or fresh from Japanese or Asian grocery stores. Japanese fish paste is the most suitable for Japanese cuisine, though it is more expensive than other fish pastes.

SERVES 4

½ carrot
200g (7oz) fish paste
2 egg yolks
1 tablespoon katakuriko *(potato starch)*
a pinch of salt
200g (7oz) winter melon, unpeeled
1 teaspoon yuzu *(Japanese citron), dry or frozen*

SOUP
4 cups (1 litre/2 pints) Katsuo Dashi (see page 144)
1 tablespoon mirin
1 tablespoon soy sauce

With a vegetable cutter, cut out the carrot to your desired shape. Slice thinly and cook in boiling water until soft. Set aside.

Place the fish paste in a bowl, add the egg yolks and mix together. Add the *katakuriko* and salt, and mix again. Divide into 4 equal portions. Roll out into small sausage shapes (3cm x 5cm/1in x 2in) to make 4 small fish cakes.

Cut the melon in half lengthways. Place the cut side down on a board and thinly slice the melon widthways, with the skin on. Take 5–7 melon slices and arrange so that they overlap slightly. Wrap the slices in a layer around a fish cake. Repeat with the remaining melon slices and fish cakes.

Set a steamer over boiling water. Place the wrapped fish cakes in the steamer and top each with a little *yuzu*. Steam over a medium heat for 20 minutes or until the winter melon skin changes colour to a brighter green.

Combine all the soup ingredients in a pan and bring to the boil.

To serve, place the wrapped fish cakes in soup bowls, seam side down, and pour the soup over. Garnish with the sliced carrot, and serve hot.

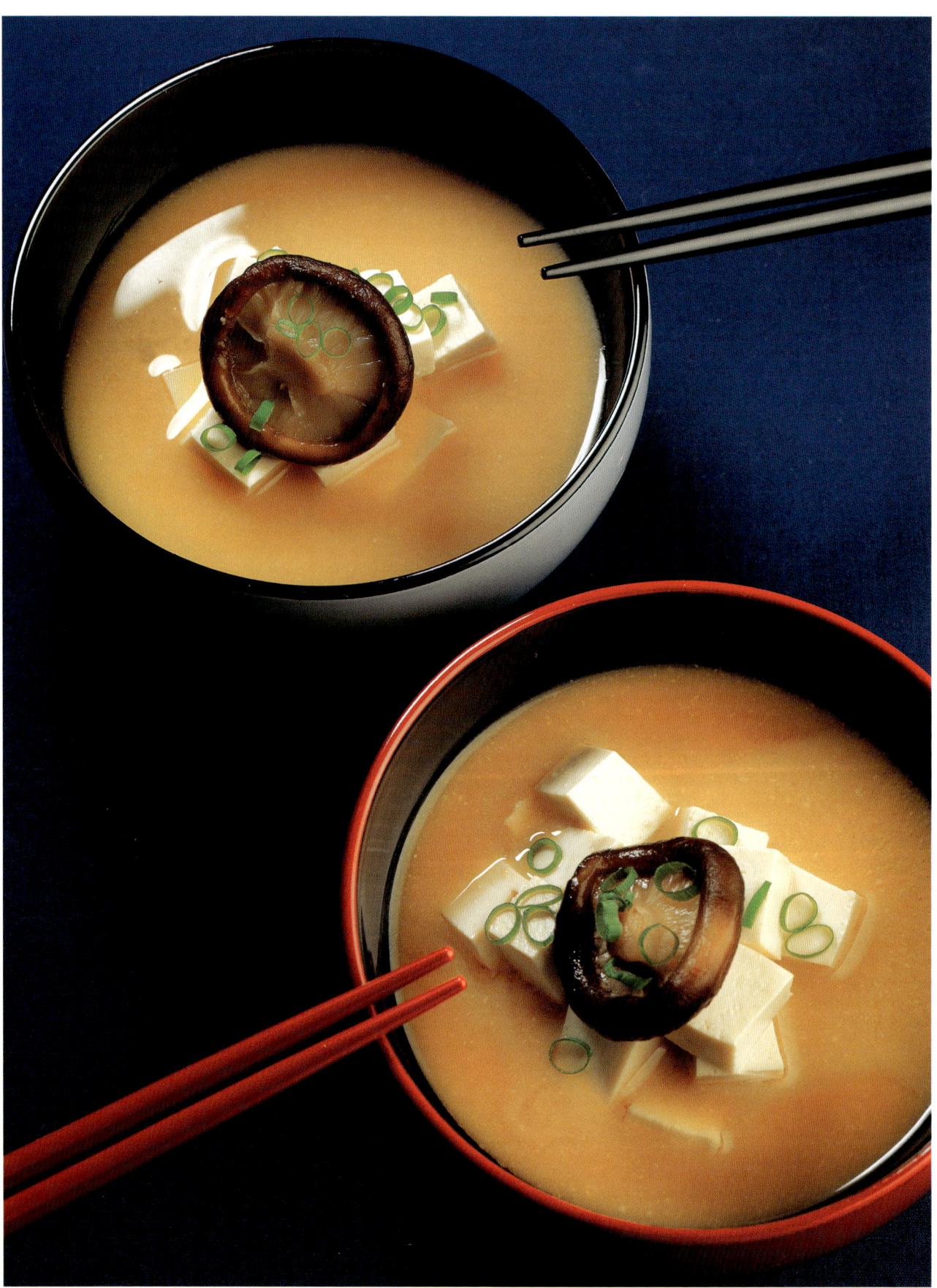

MISO SOUP WITH TŌFU AND SHĪTAKE MUSHROOMS

豆腐と椎茸の味噌汁

SERVES 4

4 dried shītake *mushrooms*
2½ cups (625ml/21fl oz) Katsuo Dashi
(see page 144)
2 tablespoons white miso
2 tablespoons red miso
1 tablespoon mirin
150g (5oz) kinugoshi-dōfu *(silken tōfu)*
1 whole spring onion (scallion), finely chopped
1 teaspoon shichimi *(Japanese seven-spice powder)*

Reconstitute the dried *shītake* mushrooms by soaking in cold water for 30 minutes or until the caps are soft. Cut and discard the stems and reserve the caps.

Place the *dashi* and mushrooms into a pan and bring to a simmer. Meanwhile, combine the white *miso*, red *miso* and *mirin* in a bowl. Add the *miso* to the *dashi* and mushrooms, and simmer until dissolved. Avoid boiling, or the soup loses its *umami* (deliciousness).

Cut the *tōfu* into 1cm (½in) cubes and add to the soup. Simmer until hot without stirring. Turn off the heat and pour the soup into serving bowls. Add the chopped spring onions as pictured opposite, and serve hot, with *shichimi*.

MISO SOUP WITH PORK LOIN AND SEASONAL VEGETABLES

豚汁

SERVES 4

4 Dutch carrots
4 baby turnips
100g (3½oz) Japanese pumpkin
6 cups (1.5 litres/3 pints) water
200g (7oz) pork loin, thinly sliced
4 tablespoons (90g/3oz) white miso
1 tablespoon mirin
3 spring onions (scallions), green part only, finely chopped
1 teaspoon shichimi *(Japanese seven-spice powder)*

Miso soup is traditionally served in small, fine-edged serving bowls. The diner holds the bowl in both hands and drinks from the bowl rather than using a spoon.

Peel and trim the carrots and turnips (see page 151). Cut the pumpkin into 4 pieces and discard the seeds. With a leaf-shaped vegetable cutter, cut out a leaf shape from each piece. If a vegetable cutter is unavailable, trim each piece into a leaf shape with a small knife (see page 151).

Bring the water to the boil in a pan. Reduce the heat, add the pork and simmer for about 30 minutes. Add the vegetables to the soup and cook over a medium heat, skimming once in a while to remove the scum.

Combine the white *miso* and *mirin* in a small bowl.

When the vegetables are soft, reduce the heat, add the *miso* and *mirin* and stir to dissolve. (If you prefer a saltier *miso*, add extra *miso* to the soup.) Turn off the heat, transfer the vegetables and pork into individual bowls and pour over the soup. Add the spring onions and serve hot with *shichimi* on the side.

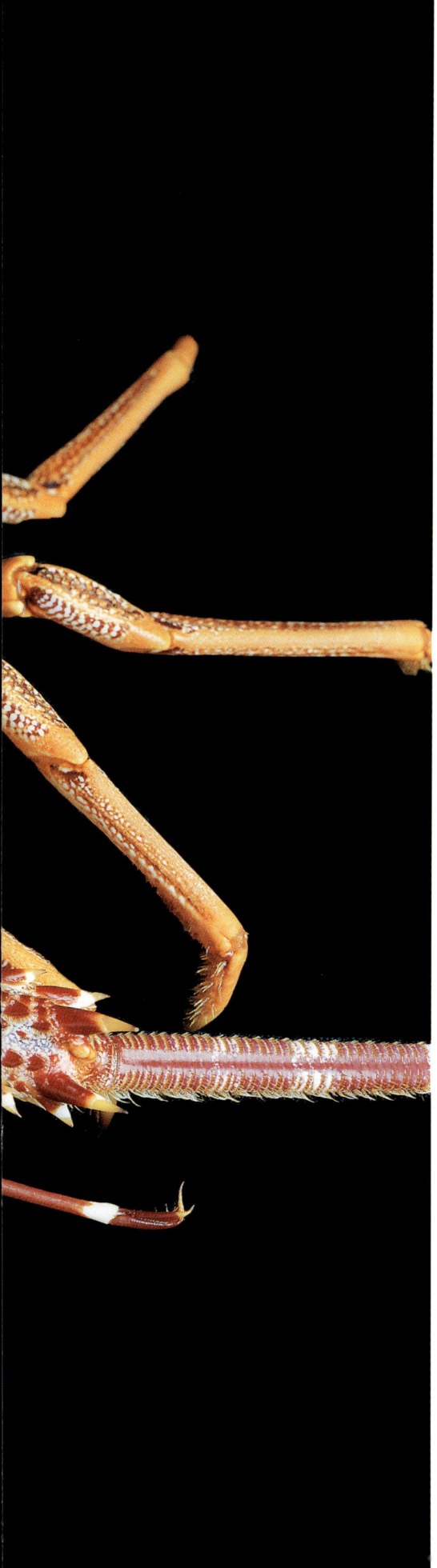

SASHIMI

Sashimi means 'sliced raw fish'. Although this is a simple dish to prepare since it needs no cooking, great care needs to be taken about the selection of fresh fish. Since the freshness of the fish is paramount, it may be worthwhile enlisting the services of a reliable fishmonger to make your selection. These days fishmongers are well aware of the special requirements of *sashimi*. White-fleshed fish are more favoured as a summer dish, while red-fleshed fish seems to be preferred in the colder seasons.

It is a good idea to take a portable esky or ice-box with you when purchasing fish for *sashimi*. Store the fish in the refrigerator, covered with cling film. It is best eaten the same day as purchased.

When slicing, use a chopping board that has been washed properly and disinfected by sunlight. A sharp knife is necessary for slicing, to prevent breaking the texture of the flesh.

Soy sauce with *wasabi* is the standard dipping sauce, and grated *daikon* or ginger are good additional condiments. Vinegar with soy sauce and hot mustard can also be used.

Refer to 'Purchasing fish for Sashimi' on page 141 before visiting your fishmonger.

COMBINATION SASHIMI ON ICE

刺身盛り合わせ

Peel the *daikon* and cut out a 10cm (4in) cylinder. Using a peeler, cut 4 ribbons about 10cm x 2.5cm (4in x 1in), along the length of the *daikon* block. Cover and refrigerate until needed.

Trim the tops and bottoms of the beetroot, and peel. Hold the beetroot in one hand, and use a peeler, or place the edge of a knife vertically on the beetroot and move it downwards in a sawing motion, to 'peel' a continuous sheet of beetroot of uniform thickness. Roll up the sheet tightly without breaking it, and cut into a thin julienne. Soak in cold water for 15 minutes, then drain. Repeat this step twice to remove some of the strong colour from the beetroot.

Trim the tuna into 4 pieces, 2.5cm (1in) square.

Place the *kombu* in a pan of water, bring it to the boil, and cook for about 10 minutes, when the *kombu* will be soft. Remove from the pan and place on a cutting board. Wipe dry, and if necessary, trim neatly into 10cm x 2.5cm (4in x 1in) rectangles. Place a rectangle of *kombu* on the board, and arrange a tuna piece on top of it at one end. Roll up the *kombu* firmly. Place a *daikon* ribbon on the board. Place the rolled *kombu* with the tuna inside it on the ribbon of *daikon*. Roll up tightly. Repeat to make 4 rolls.

Cut out 8 salmon *sashimi* slices according to the *sogi-zukuri* method (see page 149). Remove and clean heads of prawns thoroughly, leaving tails attached. Prepare the calamari according to the basic method on page 150.

Drain the shredded *daikon* and beetroot julienne. Arrange ice cubes in each bowl and place a small bamboo mat or a wire mesh on top of ice to prevent ingredients from absorbing water.

Cut each tuna roll in half widthways to make 8 pieces in total. Arrange 2 pieces of tuna roll in each serving bowl. Place 2 salmon slices, a quarter of the calamari and a cucumber crane in each bowl, and garnish with a prawn head in the centre. Top with the julienned vegetables.

Serve immediately with soy sauce and *wasabi*.

SERVES 4

1 quantity shredded daikon *(see page 152)*
1 daikon, *at least 10cm (4in) long,*
(approximately 150g/5oz), peeled
80g (2¾oz) beetroot (beets)
250g (8oz) block of sashimi-*quality tuna,*
without skin
4 pieces kombu *(kelp), 10cm x 2.5cm (4in x 1in)*
160g (5½oz) sashimi-quality salmon
2 small calamari, julienned (see page 150)
4 handfuls ice-cubes
4 cucumber cranes (see page 151)
4 medium-sized king prawns (giant shrimp),
cooked and peeled

ACCOMPANIMENTS

soy sauce
wasabi

TUNA AND SALMON SASHIMI

This classic dish showcases the freshness of the ingredients, the elegance of the presentation and the precise technique required for sashimi.

SERVES 4

1 quantity shredded daikon *(see page 152)*
2 medium-sized Lebanese cucumbers
320g (11oz) sashimi-*quality salmon fillet,*
without skin
320g (11oz) sashimi-*quality tuna fillet,*
without skin
4 sprigs bamboo
4 small edible flowers for decoration
(e.g. apple blossom)

ACCOMPANIMENTS
soy sauce
wasabi

Prepare the *daikon* according to the instructions on page 152. Carefully peel the cucumber skin the same way you peeled the *daikon*. Discard the flesh or reserve for another use. Roll up the cucumber skins gently without breaking them, and cut into a fine julienne. Soak in cold water until needed.

Run your finger along the fillets to check for bones. Remove any bones with tweezers. With a *sashimi* or filleting knife, trim the fillets, and slice in *hiki-zukuri* style (see page 149).

You should have approximately 16 pieces of *sashimi* in total.

Drain the *daikon* and cucumber and divide among the serving plates. Top each with 3–4 pieces of *sashimi*. Garnish with bamboo sprigs and flowers. Serve with soy sauce and *wasabi*.

To eat, put some *wasabi* on a piece of fish and dip in the soy sauce, or place the *wasabi* in the soy sauce and dip the *sashimi* in the sauce.

CALAMARI SASHIMI

Kuzu *is available from Japanese grocery shops. As an alternative, potato starch can be used. Calamari served in this style is meltingly tender, without a hint of rubberiness.*

In a pan, combine the *kuzu* and water and bring to a simmer while whisking. Remove the pan from the heat just before it comes to the boil. Leave to cool at room temperature until the mixture is lukewarm.

In the meantime, make cucumber string by halving and slicing the cucumber peel thinly so that it resembles string. You will need 4 strips, each about 10cm (4in) long.

Prepare calamari following the steps on page 150. Place the cleaned calamari on a board, and with a filleting knife cut into very thin julienne strips, each about the thickness of a soba noodle.

Divide the calamari julienne into four and pack into a neat row on each serving plate. Top each with a salmon strip and a cucumber string (you can interlace them as in the picture if you like). Pour the *kuzu* over the calamari and garnish with fresh lime. Serve with the dipping sauce on the side.

To make the dipping sauce, use a small leaf-shaped cutter (or knife) and make four 'leaves' of cucumber skin, as per the instructions on page 151. Make the four leaf-shaped carrot pieces in the same way, as well as four leaves of *wasabi*. You will find it easier to achieve the result if you use powdered *wasabi* mixed with a few drops of water, rather than *wasabi* from a tube.

Place a *wasabi* leaf on top of each carrot leaf, and top with a cucumber leaf. Carefully place each pile in the middle of a small dish of dipping sauce.

Alternatively, for a simpler accompaniment to the calamari, combine the juice of a lime with the soy sauce and *wasabi* to make a dipping sauce.

SERVES 4

2 teaspoons kuzu *(starch)*
1 cup (250ml/8fl oz) water
2 pieces cucumber peel, 20cm (8in) long
4 calamari, 150g (5oz) each, cleaned (see page 150)
4 thin strips salmon, 10cm (4in) long
4 lime wedges

DIPPING SAUCE

4 small leaf-shaped cucumber skins
4 small leaf-shaped carrot pieces
4 teaspoons powdered wasabi
2 tablespoons soy sauce

LOBSTERTAIL SASHIMI WITH TUNA ROLLS

ロブスター刺身

It is best to purchase a live lobster for this recipe, to ensure freshness and quality.

Place the lobster in the freezer for approximately 10 minutes to put it to sleep. Transfer the lobster to a cutting board. Cut off the head with a knife. Place the tail belly side up on the board. Cut into the belly shell and remove, leaving the tail attached. Take out the flesh and place it in iced water until it shrinks and firms up slightly.

SERVES 4

2 x 600g (20oz) lobsters
1 quantity shredded daikon *(see page 152)*
80g (2¾oz) ugo *(salted seaweed)*
4 slices lime, halved
8 inedible leaves for garnish

Prepare the shredded *daikon* according to the instructions on page 152.

To make the tuna rolls, cut *nori* to make 2 pieces measuring approximately 10cm (4in) square. Place one piece of *nori* on a cutting board (it is not necessary to use a *sudare*). Lay a strip of tuna along the bottom edge, then roll up tightly. Moisten *nori* with a wet finger to seal edges. Cut into 3 pieces. Repeat with the other half of the *nori* sheet and tuna strip.

TUNA ROLLS
half a sheet of nori
2 strips tuna, 1cm x 5cm (½in x 2in) long

To make the *wasabi* and soy sauce mixture, combine all the ingredients in a bowl and mix well.

WASABI & SOY SAUCE MIXTURE
4 tablespoons mirin
4 tablespoons soy sauce
1 teaspoon wasabi

Transfer the lobster flesh onto the cutting board and slice into *sashimi* pieces using the *hiki-zukuri* technique (see page 149). Cut pieces towards the tail slightly thicker than you slice pieces near the head.

Place each lobster shell hollow side up on a bed of *ugo*, *daikon* and 4 inedible leaves. (There is no need to cook the lobster shell.) Return the lobster flesh to the shell, and arrange lime slices at 3cm (1¼in) intervals. Top with the tuna rolls, placing them cut side up, and serve with the *wasabi* and soy sauce mixture.

Each lobster serves 2.

STEWS

Traditionally, Japanese stews contained only vegetables, though poultry and seafood were also used sparingly from time to time. This was due to the influence of Buddhism and its doctrine of respect for animal life. Today however, beef and pork are also widely used.

There are two aims when making stews. The first is the creation of palate harmony through a wise choice of ingredients, and an emphasis on the distinct flavour of each ingredient. The other is visual balance, including the preservation of the original shape of the ingredients. The ingredients, cooking style and presentation should complement each other and be representative of the season.

There are two main types of stews. One is the *takiawase* style, where more than two ingredients are cooked separately in different pots, and then served together in one dish, e.g. 'Fuki-yose Stew of Seasonal Vegetables'. The other is *nimono* style, which is when all ingredients are cooked together at the same time, e.g. 'Diced Pork in Broth'.

The primary seasonings used in Japanese stews are salt, soy sauce, *dashi* and *mirin*, which 'smooths' the flavours and adds a light glaze to the surface of the vegetables.

Even though stew is served in smaller portions in Japanese cuisine than in western cuisine, it is considered an entire course, not a side dish.

FUKI-YOSE STEW OF SEASONAL VEGETABLES

吹き寄せ煮

*Vegetables that collapse after cooking (such as potatoes), are not suitable
for this recipe. The distinctive colour of pumpkin makes it an attractive choice,
as long as the skin is left on to help the flesh keep its shape.*

Warm the *Katsuo Dashi* in a pan over low heat. Add the soy sauce, *mirin* and
sugar, and mix well. Set aside until ready to use.

SERVES 4

4 baby turnips
4 Dutch (baby) carrots
4 pieces pumpkin, each 5cm x 6cm
(2in x 2½in) of skin surface (skin on)
8 momiji *(maple leaf-shaped) carrot pieces*
(see page 151)
8 asparagus spears
4 fresh or frozen shıtake *mushrooms*
60g (2oz) fresh enoki *mushrooms*
60g (2oz) shimeji *mushrooms*

DASHI
5 cups (1.25 litres/2½ pints) Katsuo Dashi
(see page 144)
¼ cup (60ml/2fl oz) light soy sauce
1 tablespoon mirin
4 tablespoons castor sugar

With a small knife, peel the turnips from the stem to the bottom, keeping
the shape round as you go (refer to Preparation Techniques for Vegetables,
page 151). Peel and trim Dutch carrots, leaving 1cm (½in) of stem attached.

With a small knife, trim the pumpkin into a very simple leaf shape. Cut the
flesh to 1cm (½in) thickness, leaving skin attached. Using the tip of the knife
and pressing lightly, draw outlines of small shapes on the surface of the skin.
Do not cut deeply into the flesh. Using the knife, remove the skin within the
outlined areas, leaving the skin on the areas surrounding the shapes. This will
make a striking pattern on the leaf.

Place the turnips, carrot 'leaves', Dutch carrots and pumpkin 'leaves' in a
pan, and add enough water to cover. Cook over a medium heat until the
vegetables are tender, then drain.

Gently place the cooked vegetables in the *dashi*, then return the pan to the
heat and simmer for 5 minutes. Add a pinch of salt, then add the asparagus
and *shıtake* mushrooms and cook over a low heat for another 5 minutes,
without stirring.

Just before removing the pan from the heat, add the *enoki* and *shimeji*
mushrooms. Divide the vegetables among the serving bowls, pour over
the *dashi*, and serve.

ABALONE POT

あわびの貝釜

*This dish is usually cooked at the table, in front of the diners, on a hibachi
(a charcoal burner made of wood, bronze, iron, brass, copper or porcelain).
If you do not have a hibachi, cook the abalone on a wire net that has been
set over a gas ring, e.g. a small gas camping stove. There should be about
10cm (4in) clearance between the flame and the mesh.*

SERVES 4

4 slices daikon, 0.5cm (⅕in) thick
8 slices carrot, 0.5cm (⅕in) thick
4 cups (1 litre/2 pints) Kombu Dashi
(see page 144)
1 tablespoon salt
4 fresh abalone with shells, each 150g (5oz)
4 sheets kombu (kelp), each 5cm (2in) square
100g (3½oz) white miso
2 tablespoons soy sauce
2 tablespoons mirin

With a flower-shaped vegetable cutter, cut the *daikon* and carrot slices into
flower shapes.

Put the *dashi*, *daikon* and carrots into a pan, and simmer over medium heat
until the vegetables are tender. Drain the vegetables, reserving the stock.

Sprinkle salt over the abalone and leave for 10 minutes to tighten the flesh
and bring out the flavour. Rinse the abalone under running water and wipe
dry with a cloth. Insert a butter knife between the flesh and the shell, and
cut the flesh out of the shell. Place the abalone on a chopping board and,
with a sharp knife, slice thinly on an angle.

Place a *kombu* sheet inside each abalone shell. Arrange the sliced abalone
flesh on top of the *kombu*, and top with a slice each of carrot and *daikon*.
Add the *miso* and soy sauce to the *dashi* and stir until the *miso* dissolves.
Pour the *dashi* into each shell, then spoon the *mirin* over.

Heat 4 small *hibachi*. Arrange a sturdy wire mesh over each *hibachi* and place
the shells on the mesh to cook for 10–15 minutes. When the liquid reaches
the boil, the stew is ready to eat. Serve on the *hibachis*, kept at low heat.

DICED PORK IN BROTH

豚の角煮

SERVES 4

Chicken thigh fillet or lamb fillet can be substituted for pork in this recipe.

400g (14oz) pork, cut into 2.5cm (1in) cubes
1 tablespoon sake
4 tablespoons katakuriko *(potato starch)*
300ml (10fl oz) vegetable oil
4 tablespoons soy sauce
⅓ cup (90ml/3fl oz) water
2 tablespoons castor sugar
5cm (2in) piece ginger, grated
3 cloves garlic, crushed
1 tablespoon mirin
4 chive stems, sliced on a long diagonal into
5cm (2in) lengths

Place the pork in a bowl, add the *sake* and mix. Sprinkle *katakuriko* over the pork and combine.

Heat the oil in a wok or heavy-based pan to 180°C (350°F). To check the oil temperature, place a slice of garlic in the oil. If the garlic floats to the surface straightaway, the oil is ready for frying. Fry the pork, then drain it well on paper towels.

Combine the soy sauce, water, sugar, ginger and garlic in a pan and bring to the boil over a medium heat. Add the pork and simmer until the sauce is reduced and glossy. Before taking off the heat, add the *mirin* and toss to mix through. Remove the pork from the heat, garnish with the chives, and serve while hot.

GRILLS

To grill (broil) is to cook directly over or under heat, and it can be difficult to control because of uneven heat conduction. With centuries of experience in grilling, Japanese chefs have expert knowledge of what to take into account when cooking each type of ingredient. For example, in order to grill fish successfully, you must consider the texture of the flesh, the fat content and the freshness. Fish with dry flesh burns more easily than fish with moist flesh, and so needs to be cooked over a lower heat. To bring out the best in your ingredients, give some thought to their preparation and presentation. In the past, grilling techniques were quite limited. These days, there are several styles, including 'teriyaki style' (e.g. Eel Teriyaki, page 71), 'salted grill' (e.g. Spring Dish, page 9) and 'skewered grill', pictured left.

GRILLED SQUID WITH HŌBA LEAF

いかの化粧焼き

Choose the very freshest squid for this recipe. This dish is traditionally cooked on a hibachi *at the final stage, though you could use a small camping stove or barbecue instead. In case you don't have access to any of these, complete directions for oven grilling have also been included.*

Clean the squid following the instructions on page 150. Discard the tentacles. Make light diagonal cuts on one side of the squid at 1cm (½in) intervals (be careful not to cut through the flesh). Repeat to make a crosshatch pattern.

SERVES 4

4 squid tubes, 100g (3½oz) each, cleaned (see page 150)
4 teaspoons mirin
4 tablespoons salted butter
2 quantities Egg Mimosa (see page 146)
4 leaves mitsuba *(trefoil), finely chopped*
4 dried hōba *leaves or 4 pieces dried or fresh banana leaves*

Sprinkle *mirin* over the squid and top each tube with 1 tablespoon butter. Grill (broil) the squid lightly on one side under an oven griller. If you do not have a *hibachi*, turn the squid at this point and grill the other side. Test with a skewer to determine when the squid is cooked: it should still be moist and tender with some juices.

If you plan to use a *hibachi*, do not turn the squid over; top the grilled side with Egg Mimosa and a *mitsuba* leaf, and return to the grill. If using an oven grill only, carry out this stage only after both sides have been grilled. When the Egg Mimosa turns golden brown, transfer each squid onto a *hōba* leaf, mimosa side up. If you are using the oven grill method only, both sides will be cooked and the squid will be ready to serve.

ACCOMPANIMENT
4 tablespoons soy sauce

Otherwise, light the *hibachi* using a solid fuel such as heat beads, and place the *hōba* leaves on the *hibachi* to cook the underside. As with the oven grill method, test the squid with a skewer to determine when it is cooked: it should still be moist and tender with some juices. Serve immediately on the *hibachi* with the heat kept low.

Offer soy sauce separately.

GRILLED GARFISH WITH MUSHROOMS

Nameko *and* shimeji *mushrooms are available from selected greengrocers and Asian grocery shops. They are usually available only in season (autumn) but at other times of the year, cultivated mushrooms can be used instead.*

Preheat the oven to 180°C (350°F).

SERVES 4

4 whole garfish, about 30cm (12in) long from beak to tail

100g (3½ oz) nameko *or* enoki *mushrooms*

100g (3½ oz) shimeji *mushrooms*

2 tablespoons mirin

2 teaspoons white sesame seeds

4 chives

ACCOMPANIMENT

soy sauce

With a sharp filleting knife, remove the garfish heads and rinse fish under running water. To fillet the garfish, run the knife along the spine of the fish from the head towards the tail. Turn the fish over and repeat on the other side. Remove tails from skeleton and set aside.

Place the fillet, skin side down, on a board. Place the *nameko* or *enoki* and *shimeji* mushrooms across the fillet, leaving the caps sticking out one side. Place the garfish tail on top of the caps, with most of the tail sticking out, and roll the fillet up tightly. Secure the end with a toothpick. Sprinkle *mirin* and white sesame seeds over the fish.

Place the rolled fish on a baking tray and bake until the flesh turns white. This should take about 6 minutes.

To serve, transfer 2 rolled garfish onto each plate and remove the toothpicks. Tuck the chives behind the mushrooms and serve with soy sauce.

UNAGI NO KABAYAKI (EEL TERIYAKI)

鰻の蒲焼

In Japan, eel is favoured as a summer dish. When purchasing, choose a short black-fin eel (Japanese eel). Pre-cooked or vacuum-sealed eel is available from Japanese stores and some Asian stores. Live or fresh eel is available from some fish markets or fishmongers. Ask your fishmonger to fillet the eel but get the head and bones too, as they are useful for making stocks and sauces. Try to use charcoal when making this dish, as its aroma enhances the flavour of the eel, particularly as the teriyaki sauce drips down onto the hot coals.

SERVES 4

400g (14oz) fresh eel fillet
sanshō *pepper*
1 sprig kinome *(young* sanshō *leaves)*

TERIYAKI SAUCE
2 tablespoons mirin
1 cup (250ml/8fl oz) soy sauce
1 cup (250g/8oz) rock crystal sugar
eel head and bones

To make *teriyaki* sauce, place the *mirin*, soy sauce and rock crystal sugar in a pan and mix. Add the eel head and bones, and simmer over a medium heat until the mixture has reduced and thickened to a sauce. Remove from the heat.

Place the fillet on a board, skin side down. Using 2 bamboo skewers or stainless steel skewers, skewer the eel along the skin side.

Grill (broil) the eels directly on a large *hibachi* or barbecue over a medium heat, turning and basting both sides with the sauce at least 10 times during cooking. Be careful not to scorch the eels too much.

Before serving, remove the skewers and place on a plate, skin side down. Serve whole or cut into bite-sized pieces, sprinkled with *sanshō* pepper and garnished with *kinome*.

Rice is a good accompaniment to grilled eel.

GRILLED SALMON WITH ROASTED RICE

サーモンの焼き物

This dish lets the beautiful translucent colour of salmon flesh speak for itself. The fillet must be cut from a large fish as the piece needs to be at least 5cm (2in) thick. If pre-packaged dōmyōji-ko is unavailable, you can make your own at home, though it is difficult to achieve the same effect. Rinse and steam short grain rice until soft, then scatter the cooked grains on an oven tray and roast at about 200°C (400°F) until crisp.

SERVES 4

400g (14oz) thick salmon fillet, skin on
4 teaspoons sake
2 egg yolks, beaten
2 pinches of salt
4 teaspoon yukari
4 tablespoons roasted dōmyōji-ko
(crushed sticky rice)
red shiso leaves for garnish

ACCOMPANIMENT
soy sauce

Place the salmon on a board, skin side down, and slicing across the whole fillet, cut into 4 pieces about 3cm (1¼ in) wide. Turn the pieces skin side up. Make a horizontal cut along the centre of each piece to a depth of 1cm (½ in). Cover an oven tray with foil and place the salmon pieces on it, skin side up. Sprinkle with sake. Brush egg yolk over the skin and sprinkle with salt.

Grill (broil) the fish at a medium heat until medium rare (this should take no more than 15 minutes). Take the tray out of the griller (broiler) and sprinkle over the *yukari* and roasted *dōmyōji-ko*. Return to the griller, and grill at a low heat until the *dōmyōji-ko* is scorched.

Transfer the fish onto serving plates, garnish with red *shiso* and serve with soy sauce.

YOSEMONO

Yosemono is a savoury Japanese dish of vegetables or seafood cooked in *dashi* and set in *kanten* (agar-agar). It is a unique Japanese dish that is difficult to translate directly into English. 'Pudding' is the closest translation, but it is not a pudding in the English sense of the word—it is like a savoury aspic, set with agar-agar (a marine plant) rather than an animal extract. Since *yosemono* is a delicate dish with a simple and fragile taste, it is important to cook it with a delicate touch.

寄せもの

GREEN TEA TŌFU

抹茶豆腐

SERVES 4

2 tablespoons kanten (agar-agar) powder
1 tablespoon water
300g (10oz) silken tōfu (kinugoshi-dōfu)
3 tablespoons matcha (green tea) powder
4 nori sheet strips, 3cm x 25cm (1in x 10in)
4 cumquat slices
4 spring onion (scallion) stems, blanched
and knotted

DIPPING SAUCE
3 tablespoons Katsuo Dashi (see page 144)
3 tablespoons mirin
3 tablespoons soy sauce

ACCOMPANIMENT
40g (1½oz) ginger, peeled and grated

Dissolve the kanten powder in the water.

Mash the tōfu in a pan using a potato masher. Add the matcha powder
and stir until well combined. Heat the tōfu mixture until warm and add
the kanten, mixing until dissolved. Strain the mixture through a sieve into
a rectangular mould approximately 7cm x 30cm (3in x 12in) and refrigerate
for 30 minutes or until set.

To make the dipping sauce, combine the dashi, mirin and soy sauce in
a bowl.

When firmly set, remove the mould from the fridge and run a knife
around the edges to loosen the jelly. Invert onto a board and cut into
5cm (2in) squares.

Place a square in each small bowl. Wrap a strip of nori around the bottom
of each square and top with a cumquat slice and a knotted spring onion.
Serve chilled with the dipping sauce and grated ginger.

ASPARAGUS AND KING PRAWN ASPIC

アスパラガスと海老の寄せもの

Soak the *kanten* powder in the water.

Cut the asparagus into 3cm (1¼in) pieces and blanch in a pot of boiling water for 1 minute. Remove from the heat, drain and set aside.

Thread a bamboo skewer along the belly of each prawn, from the head towards the tail. Bring a pot of water to the boil and blanch the prawns until the shells turn red. Drain the prawns, then refresh them under running water. Peel the prawns, remove the skewers and set aside.

SERVES 4

2 tablespoons kanten *(agar-agar) powder*
1 tablespoon water
4 asparagus spears
4 king prawns (giant shrimp)
4 satoimo *(taro), whole and peeled*
1 cup (250ml/8fl oz) Katsuo Dashi *(see page 144)*
2 tablespoons soy sauce
1 tablespoon mirin

Bring a fresh pot of water to the boil, reduce the heat, then simmer the *satoimo* until soft. Remove from the heat, drain then mash the *satoimo*. Push the mash through a fine sieve.

Combine the *dashi*, soy sauce and *mirin* in a pan and heat over a low flame. Remove the pan from the heat before the liquid comes to the boil. Add the *kanten* and stir until dissolved. Pour the mixture into the *satoimo* and mix together with a spatula.

Pour half the mixture into a rectangular mould measuring approximately 7cm × 20cm (3in × 8in) and refrigerate for 3 minutes.

Remove the mould from the refrigerator and place a layer of asparagus on the *dashi* layer. Place a layer of prawns on top of the asparagus. Pour the rest of the *dashi* over the asparagus and prawns, and refrigerate for 1 hour.

When firmly set, remove the mould from the fridge and run a knife around the edges to loosen the jelly. Invert onto a board, slice and serve.

SATOIMO AND SPINACH CROWN

里芋とほうれん草の寄せもの

Soak the *kanten* powder in the water.

Trim the *satoimo* by cutting off the bottom and top to make a cylinder. With a round cutter of about 2.5cm (1in) in diameter, cut out a piece from the *satoimo*. Make 4 barrels in the same way.

SERVES 4

2 tablespoons kanten *(agar-agar) powder*
2 tablespoons water
4 satoimo *(taro)*
3 cups (750ml/24fl oz) Katsuo Dashi
(see page 144)
1 tablespoon soy sauce
a pinch of salt
1 tablespoon mirin
1 bunch English spinach
1 tablespoon salt
1 okra, thinly sliced

ACCOMPANIMENT
soy sauce

Place the *satoimo* in a pan with enough *dashi* to cover. Make sure you don't use all the *dashi*. Bring to the boil and simmer until the *satoimo* are soft. Add the soy sauce, salt and *mirin*, and remove from the heat.

Rinse the spinach under running water. Bring some salted water to the boil and blanch the spinach. Drain, then refresh under cold running water. Squeeze dry and purée.

Reheat the remaining *dashi* in a pan. When it comes to the boil, remove it from the heat and add the *kanten*, stirring until dissolved. Add the spinach to the *dashi* and mix together gently.

Pour the mixture into a rectangular mould or tin measuring approximately 10cm x 20cm/4in x 8in, and evenly space the *satoimo* barrels in a row down the middle. Refrigerate until firm.

When firmly set, remove the mould from the fridge and run a knife around the edges to loosen the jelly. Invert onto a board and with a flower-shaped cutter, cut out 4 flowers, centring the *satoimo* in the cutter.

To serve, place a flower in each bowl and top with a slice of raw okra. Serve with soy sauce on the side.

AGEMONO

Agemono generally means 'fried food'. This includes foods fried with a coating of breadcrumbs, flour or tempura batter. *Tempura* is a Japanese style of deep-frying. Good *tempura* is characterised by a crispy and light batter. It is crucial that clean vegetable oil and fresh ingredients are used, and that the *tempura* is well drained so that it is not too oily and heavy.

In earlier times, sesame oil was used instead of vegetable oil. Nowadays vegetable oil is used and just a few drops of sesame oil are added for additional flavour.

After draining the *tempura* properly on a rack or paper towels, it is recommended that you serve it on *kaishi* (Japanese paper) or paper towel to absorb the last of the oil. *Tempura* should be served warm, while still crispy, with a dipping sauce or salt.

Popular condiments to have with *tempura* include *daikon-oroshi* (grated *daikon*), thinly sliced *myōga* (Japanese ginger) and lemon wedges.

A new style of deep-fried dish is also introduced in this chapter: deep-fried *tempura* wrapped with kelp or crushed *harusame* (Japanese vermicelli). Once you have mastered the *tempura* technique you might enjoy experimenting with your own ideas to create a new style.

KING PRAWNS WITH SEASONAL VEGETABLE TEMPURA

海老の変わり揚げと季節の野菜の天ぷら

To make the *matcha* salt, combine the *matcha* powder and salt. Set aside. Carve patterns on the squash with a small knife. Set aside until ready to use. Rinse the *nanohana*, drain well on paper towels and set aside. Peel the prawns, leaving the tails on. De-vein with the tip of a knife, discard the digestive tract and rinse under running water. Drain and wipe dry. Cut off the tip of the tails and force out any excess moisture by pressing on the prawns with the back of a knife.

Holding prawns by the tail, lightly coat 4 prawns with *katakuriko*. Rinse the *kombu* and wipe dry. Place on a board and fold each in half. Using scissors or a sharp knife, cut slits running from the fold to within 1cm (⅛in) of the fore edge, all the way across (make a cut at about every 0.5cm/⅛in interval). Take 4 prawns and place each one inside a piece of *kombu*, the head towards the fold, the tail sticking out. Tie the ends of each sheet together around the tail with a strip of *kanpyō* and set aside.

To prepare the batter, mix the egg yolk and iced water in a bowl. Add flour and combine lightly. The mixture will still be a little lumpy. Set aside. The batter may be made ahead of time, but must be refrigerated until use. Place the flour in a tray and coat the remaining 4 prawns. Wrap a *nori* strip around each tail joint, sealing the ends with a little drop of water. Spread the crushed *harusame* in a tray. Holding the prawn tail, dip each prawn in the batter and transfer to the *harusame*. With your fingers, press the *harusame* onto the prawn, leaving the tail free.

Heat the vegetable oil in a wok or frying pan to 170°C (340°F) and add the sesame oil. Deep-fry prawns in *harusame* until the *harusame* puffs up. Remove and drain on paper towels or a rack. Deep-fry prawns in *kombu* until crisp. Remove and drain on paper towels or a rack. Coat *nanohana* stems with flour and dip in the batter. Deep-fry quickly, and drain on paper towels or a rack. To deep-fry whole *harusame* noodles, place 2 noodles at a time in the oil and fry quickly. Remove when the *harusame* becomes puffy (a few seconds), then drain as above. Deep-fry the squash in the oil.

To serve, place 1 *kombu* prawn and 1 *harusame* prawn on each serving plate, add 1 stem of *nanohana*, 1 squash and 2 *harusame* noodles. Serve warm with *matcha* salt alongside for dipping, or sprinkled over each plate.

SERVES 4

4 squash
4 stems nanohana (canola)
8 fresh king prawns (giant shrimp),
no longer than 15cm (6in)
4 tablespoons katakuriko (potato starch)
4 sheets kombu, 16cm x 3cm (6in x 1½in)
4 strips kanpyō, 10cm (4in) long
¼ cup (75g/2½oz) plain flour
4 strips nori, 1cm x 5cm (½in x 2in) long
100g (3½oz) harusame (vermicelli), crushed
vegetable oil for deep-frying
a few drops of sesame oil
8 whole harusame noodles

MATCHA SALT
1 tablespoon matcha (green tea) powder
1 tablespoon salt

BATTER MIXTURE
1 egg yolk
½ cup (125ml/4fl oz) iced water
1 cup (250g/8oz) plain flour

DEEP-FRIED KING PRAWNS WITH BREADCRUMBS AND EGG MIMOSA

海老の黄身揚げ

Combine the breadcrumbs and Egg Mimosa in a tray and set aside.

SERVES 4

2 cups (120g/4oz) breadcrumbs
4 quantities Egg Mimosa (see page 147)
8 king prawns (giant shrimp)
extra plain flour
8 strips nori, *each 1cm x 6cm (½in x 2½in)*
300ml (10fl oz) vegetable oil
4 lime wedges
4 spring onion (scallion) stems with
edible flower, for garnish

BATTER
1 egg yolk
180ml (6fl oz) iced water
2 cups (250g/8oz) plain flour

Peel the prawns and remove the heads, but leave the tails on. De-vein with the tip of a knife, discard the digestive tract and rinse under running water. Drain and wipe dry. Cut off the tips of the tails and force out any excess moisture by pressing on the prawns with the back of a knife.

To make the batter, mix the egg yolk and iced water in a bowl. Add the flour, combining lightly with chopsticks or a fork. The batter will be a little lumpy. Keep the batter in the refrigerator until you are ready to use it.

Place the extra flour in a tray and use to coat the prawns. Wrap each tail joint with a *nori* strip, sealing the ends with a drop of water.

Heat the oil in a wok or frying pan to 180°C (350°F).

Holding onto the prawn tail, dip each prawn in batter, then coat with the breadcrumb mixture. Deep-fry until golden brown. Drain on paper towels or a rack.

Garnish with an edible flower and a lime wedge. Serve immediately.

SATSUMA-AGE (DEEP-FRIED FISH CAKES) WITH SHĪTAKE MUSHROOMS

薩摩揚げ

Satsuma-age *is a deep-fried fish cake made from fish paste. Fish paste is quite readily available from Asian grocery shops or fishmongers or you can make your own: in a food processor, mix white-fleshed fish (such as snapper or cuttlefish) and blend until a paste forms.*

SERVES 4

8 dried shıtake *mushrooms*
2 tablespoons mirin
a pinch of salt
4 tablespoons soy sauce
3 egg yolks
4 tablespoons katakuriko *(potato starch)*
200g (7oz) fish paste, frozen
8 chives, finely chopped
extra katakuriko
300ml (10fl oz) vegetable oil
4 red radishes, grated
soy sauce

Reconstitute the dried *shıtake* mushrooms by soaking in some warm water until the caps are soft. Cut and discard the stems and reserve the caps. Using a flower-shaped vegetable cutter, cut out a flower shape from each mushroom.

To make the fish cakes, combine the *mirin*, salt, soy sauce, egg yolks and *katakuriko* in a large bowl. Add the fish paste and chives, and mix well with a wooden spoon, ensuring that the ingredients are well amalgamated.

Dust your hands with extra *katakuriko*. Take a tablespoon of the mixture and roll to form a round ball. Press it flat, and place a *shıtake* mushroom in the middle. Push the *shıtake* into the cake to ensure that it sticks. Repeat with the remaining mixture. You should have 8 fish cakes.

Heat the oil in a wok or frying pan to 180°C (350°F). Deep-fry the fish cakes until golden brown. Drain on paper towels or a rack.

Serve immediately with grated radish and soy sauce.

SUSHI

Sushi is one of the better known dishes of Japanese cuisine, as popular abroad as it is in Japan. In this seemingly simple dish—essentially little more than small parcels of rice with a topping—lies the beauty and grace of Japanese food. Sushi showcases the versatility of Japanese cuisine, and is frequently regarded as the 'dish of dishes'.

A great deal of importance is placed upon the preparation of rice for sushi (see page 146). The technique used in washing the rice at the beginning determines the end result as much as the way the rice is cooked thereafter. As one complements the other, I place great importance on correct technique.

It might not be an exaggeration to say that there is nothing to beat sushi-making for fun in Japanese cooking, once you have mastered the skills. Using a sudare (sushi mat), you can create a variety of shapes, from a cylinder-shaped roll to a square roll. The ingredients chosen for sushi depend on the season, with exceptional freshness the only requirement.

The most highly regarded type of sushi, the province of master chefs, is nigiri-zushi (moulded sushi). There is almost a rhythm to how the sushi is made. First the chef dips his hands into water and then claps hard to remove the excess water. Then the chef grasps a little sushi rice with one hand and simultaneously moulds it into a finger shape. A little wasabi is smeared onto the rice and a topping of hand-sliced raw fish is placed on top. The sushi is then transferred onto a plate. Not everyone can make sushi like these nigiri chefs, but every nigiri has its own charms.

NIGIRI-ZUSHI TECHNIQUE
握り寿司の作り方

MAKES 14 PIECES OF NIGIRI-ZUSHI

14 pieces of **sogi-zukuri** *sliced fish, calamari, cuttlefish, sliced grilled eel,
flattened prawn or avocado*
3 cups cooked **Sushi** *Rice (see page 146)*
1 cup (250ml/8fl oz) water
1 teaspoon vinegar

Prepare 14 pieces of fish such as tuna, salmon or snapper using the *sogi-zukuri*
slicing technique (see page 149). Calamari, cuttlefish, sliced grilled eel (see
page 71), a flattened king prawn or slices of avocado work well too.

Have the sliced ingredients ready and a dry board in front of you.
Combine water and vinegar in a bowl. Wash your hands well, dip your
fingers into the bowl of vinegared water, then clap your hands together
to remove any excess water.

Pick up a slice of fish with your right hand and place it in your left, which is
slightly cupped to hold the fish. (Reverse the hands if you are left-handed.)
Using the tip of your right index finger, take a little *wasabi* and smear it on
the fish.

With the fish in your left hand, grasp a little rice with your right hand. Rest
the rice on the base of your fingers and squeeze lightly to form the rice into
an oval-shaped pillow. Neaten the shape by turning the rice pillow around
and pressing gently.

Transfer the rice onto the fish and press the fish and rice together. Hold your
right index and middle fingers straight out together and place over the *sushi*,
then gently press. Turn over so the rice is now on top and gently press again.
Turn over so the fish is on top again and press once more to complete.

Sushi is usually served with pickled ginger, and soy sauce for dipping.

NORI ROLL TECHNIQUE

巻き寿司の作り方

MAKES 2 ROLLS/12 PIECES

1 cup cooked Sushi *Rice (see page 146)*
1 sheet nori, *cut in half lengthways*
2 teaspoons wasabi
half a cucumber, seeded and cut into strips 1cm (½in) wide

DIPPING WATER
1 cup (250ml/8fl oz) water
1 teaspoon rice vinegar

This is a basic technique for nori *rolls using cucumber. For a successful result, spread a handful of rice thinly over the* nori *without squashing it down. Do not put too much rice or ingredients on the* nori. *Instead of cucumber, pickled daikon or cooked asparagus can be used.*

To make the dipping water, combine the water and rice vinegar in a bowl.

Place a *sushi* mat on a flat surface and put a sheet of *nori* on top, glossy side down. Moisten your fingers with the dipping water. Using your fingers, spread the *sushi* rice over the bottom two-thirds of the nori, to the edges, leaving the top third uncovered. Spread *wasabi* across the centre of the rice and top with strips of cucumber placed in a line.

Lift the edge of the *sushi* mat and roll up, pushing the rice and cucumber inside with the tips of your fingers. Gently but firmly roll the *sushi* in the mat to form a round shape. Unroll the mat and remove the *sushi* roll to a dry board. Repeat with the rest of the ingredients.

Wipe a knife with a wet cloth. Cut the rolls in half. Arrange the two halves next to each other and cut both rolls into 3 pieces simultaneously, to make 6 pieces. Clean the knife between cuttings.

NIGIRI-ZUSHI
(HAND-MOULDED SUSHI)

握り寿司

This dish presents three different examples of the revered art of nigiri-zushi.

Divide the *sushi* rice into 3 batches.

SERVES 4

2 cups cooked Sushi *Rice (see page 146)*
1 teaspoon wasabi, *placed in a small bowl*
9 chives, trimmed to 12cm (5in) length
8 slices salmon, cut using the sogi-zukuri
method (see page 149)
1 sheet nori, *cut lengthways into*
1cm (½in) wide strips
6 slices cuttlefish, cut using the sogi-zukuri
method (see page 149)
1 teaspoon vinegar
1 cup (250ml/8fl oz) water
caviar for garnish
4 sanshō *leaves for garnish*
soy sauce

MANGO SAUCE
half a ripe mango
a drop of rice vinegar or white vinegar
a drop of mirin

To make the salmon *nigiri-zushi* (pictured top), use one batch of *sushi* rice and follow the instructions for making *nigiri* rice 'pillows' on page 92. Hold the chives together in a neat, tight bunch and cut into 3cm (1in) lengths, keeping the 4 small bunches separate. Top each *nigiri* with one small bunch of chives laid flat lengthways. Continue following the instructions for making *nigiri-zushi* using sliced salmon on page 92. Wrap a *nori* strip around the middle of the *sushi* and cut in half along the middle of the *nori* strip with a clean, sharp knife.

To make the cuttlefish *nigiri-zushi* (pictured middle), follow the instructions for preparing cuttlefish for *nigiri-zushi* on page 150. Then, using one remaining batch of *sushi* rice, follow the instructions for making *nigiri-zushi* on page 92. Garnish with caviar.

To make the *Nimaizuke nigiri-zushi* (pictured bottom left), fold a slice of salmon in half vertically in the palm of your hand. Place a slice of cuttlefish on top of the salmon, making sure the left side of both is flush. Follow the instructions for making *nigiri-zushi* on page 92, then place a *sanshō* leaf on top of the *sushi*.

To make the mango sauce, peel the mango and purée the flesh in a blender. Add the rice vinegar and *mirin* and blend for 20 seconds. Spoon a little mango sauce over the cuttlefish *nigiri-zushi*. (Mango sauce is suitable for serving with white-fleshed fish or shellfish in *sushi* or *sashimi*.)

Serve with soy sauce on the side.

KAKUMAKI (SQUARE NORI ROLL)

Using a flower-shaped cutter no bigger than a small coin, cut out 4 *daikon* 'flowers'. Place 'flowers' in a bowl of iced water until ready to use. To make the omelette, heat an omelette pan with a drop of oil over medium heat, and pour in half the eggs. Swirl to cover, as if making a thin crêpe. When the surface becomes dry, transfer to a plate. Repeat with the remainder of the eggs. Trim the omelettes to 20cm x 20cm (8in x 8in) and set aside.

To make the red rice, cook the raw rice with the food colouring following the instructions for cooking *sushi* rice (see page 146).

Place a full-sized *nori* sheet glossy side down. Place a few grains of sushi rice along one of the longer edges. Place the long edge of a ⅔-sized *nori* sheet over this, glossy side down with centrepoints of both pieces aligned and the pieces overlapping by 0.5–1 cm (¼in–½in). Spread the red rice thinly over the ⅔-sized sheet and the white rice over the full-sized *nori* sheet. Starting from the red rice side, roll both sheets of *nori* into a tight cylinder. Cut the roll in half lengthways, and cut each halved roll in half, lengthwise again, to make 4 long strips.

Join the long edges of 2 full-sized *nori* sheets with a little *sushi* rice. Place on a *sushi* mat, glossy side down. Place the omelette in the middle of the sheet. Place 2 quarters of the sliced *sushi* roll flat side down with nori edges touching, over the join in the unrolled *nori* sheets. Top with *takuan*, then the remaining 2 quarters of the *sushi* roll, flat side up with nori edges against the *takuan*. Lift the edge of the *sushi* mat and roll up to enclose the filling and form a square 'log'. Gently but firmly press the mat around the roll to set the shape. Unroll the mat and transfer the *sushi* roll to a dry board. Repeat with the rest of the ingredients. Wipe a knife with a wet towel. Cut each roll across into 8 pieces, cleaning the knife between cuts.

To serve, arrange 4 pieces on a plate and top each with a *daikon* 'flower'. Place a salmon egg in the middle of each *daikon* 'flower'.

SERVES 4

4 *thin slices* daikon
6 *full-sized sheets* nori *(20cm x 18cm/8in x 7in)*
1 cup cooked Sushi *Rice (see page 146)*
2 ⅔-*size sheets* nori *(20cm x 12cm/8in x 5in)*
2 takuan *(pickled radish), cut into*
2cm x 2cm x 20cm (¾in x ¾in x 8in) pieces
2 *tablespoons salmon caviar*

THIN OMELETTE
2 *eggs, beaten*
2 *drops vegetable oil*

RED RICE
1 cup (220g/7oz) raw short-grain rice
1 drop natural red food colouring

DIPPING WATER
1 cup (250ml/8fl oz) water
1 teaspoon white vinegar

Tazuna-zushi (Twisted Rope Sushi)

手綱寿司

To make the *Sushi* Rice, follow the instructions on page 146. Allow the rice to cool to room temperature.

To make the dipping water, combine the two ingredients in a bowl.

To prepare the king prawns, use a bamboo skewer to skewer each prawn from head to tail along the back vein so that it is held out straight. Cook in boiling water with a pinch of salt for 3 minutes. Drain, then cool under running water. Peel each prawn and remove the head. Make a deep slit down the underside of each prawn, and spread open like a butterfly.

To prepare the roll, cut out 3 pieces of cling film exactly the size of the *sushi* mat. Working with 1 sheet at a time, place the wrap on the mat. Arrange 2 cuttlefish slices, 2 butterflied king prawns and a salmon slice diagonally across the centre of the cling wrap as pictured, each piece just touching the next. Place the spring onion stems between each slice.

With moist hands, spread a handful of *sushi* rice evenly over the slices. Hold the edge of the mat and fold in half. Push firmly with your hands to form a neat cylinder. Unroll the mat and transfer the *sushi* to a dry board.

Repeat with the remaining two pieces of cling film and the rest of the ingredients.

Wipe a knife with a wet cloth. Remove the cling film and cut each *sushi* roll widthways into 3 pieces, cleaning the knife between cuttings. Gently press one end of each piece into the Egg Mimosa to coat.

Serve with soy sauce and *wasabi*.

MAKES 9 PIECES

3 cups cooked Sushi Rice *(see page 146)*
6 slices cuttlefish (see page 150)
6 king prawns (giant shrimp)
3 slices salmon, cut using the sogi-zukuri
method (see page 150)
6 spring onion (scallion) stems
1 quantity Egg Mimosa (see page 147)
soy sauce
wasabi

DIPPING WATER
1 cup (250ml/8fl oz) water
1 teaspoon vinegar

CHIRASHI-ZUSHI (SCATTERED SUSHI)

To make the *sushi* rice, follow the instructions on page 146. Allow the rice to cool to room temperature.

SERVES 4

3 cups cooked Sushi Rice *(see page 146)*
80g (2¾oz) benishōga *(red pickled ginger), chopped*
4 small cuttlefish tubes, cleaned (see page 150)
4 teaspoons goma-shio *(roasted black sesame seeds with salt)*
32 pieces sashimi *salmon, cut using the* sogi-zukuri *method (see page 149)*
4 teaspoons wasabi
32 capers
2 quantities Egg Mimosa (see page 147)
4 medium-sized king prawns (giant shrimp), cooked and peeled, with heads left on
4 tablespoons soy sauce
inedible green leaves (e.g. bamboo), for decoration

Divide the cooled rice into 2 batches. Transfer one batch to a mixing bowl, add the *benishōga* and combine with a wet rice ladle.

Divide the *benishōga sushi* rice among 4 glass bowls to a depth of 1.5cm (⅗in). Divide the other batch of plain *sushi* rice among the 4 bowls, on top of the *benishōga sushi* rice, to the same depth. This will create 2 contrasting layers of rice. Sprinkle over the *goma-shio*.

Clean the cuttlefish following the instructions on page 150. Wipe the cuttlefish dry with a cloth or paper towels. Cut open the tubes, fold in half and slice each tube into 5 strips. Roll up each slice of cuttlefish.

Place a slice of salmon on the board, put a rolled cuttlefish on top and fold in half to enclose. Repeat with the remaining cuttlefish and salmon.

Arrange 8 pieces of salmon roll on top of the rice in each bowl, with the open ends facing towards the centre of each bowl like the petals of a flower. Dab a little *wasabi* on each piece of salmon and cuttlefish roll. Place a caper on top of each roll. Arrange a little Egg Mimosa in the centre of the bowl like a flower pistil. Stand the prawn on the Egg Mimosa with its head pointing up. Garnish with green leaves and serve with soy sauce and *wasabi*.

SALADS AND PICKLES

Japanese salad is quite similar to western salad, consisting of tossed vegetables and other ingredients with a dressing. The dressing may also be served on the side. A feature of Japanese salad is the dressing ingredients, which usually contain soy sauce, vegetable oil, *wasabi*, *miso* or *mirin*.

Many Japanese pickling techniques have been handed down from generation to generation. Furthermore, each region has its own unique produce, and the pickles tend to make use of these local ingredients. Recently a health issue arose within the Japanese community, over the high salt content of pickles. To remedy the situation, salt-reduced pickles have been introduced.

TOMATO AND CALAMARI SALAD WITH SHISO-UME PURÉE

トマトとイカのサラダ

Yukari *(dried, flaked shiso) can be used instead of fresh* shiso *leaves if necessary.*

SERVES 4

3 small calamari tubes, cleaned (see page 150)
12 cherry (cocktail) tomatoes
4 red or green shiso *leaves, finely chopped or*
4 pinches yukari
1 onion, finely chopped
12 kaiware *(radish sprouts)*

SHISO-UME PURÉE
4 tablespoons shiso-ume *(Japanese plum paste)*
1 teaspoon olive oil
juice of 1 lemon
1 teaspoon soy sauce

Rinse the cleaned calamari tubes under running water and blanch in a pot of salted boiling water. Drain, then refresh with cold water and refrigerate.

Blanch the tomatoes in boiling salted water. Remove and transfer to a bowl of cold water until cool. Peel.

To make the *shiso-ume* purée, combine the *shiso-ume* and olive oil in a small bowl and whisk. Add the lemon juice and soy sauce, then whisk until well combined.

Cut each calamari open to make a sheet. Trim into a rectangular shape by cutting the top edge in a straight line. Slice each calamari sheet widthways into 4 strips. Roll each strip of calamari into a cylinder.

Place 3 calamari 'cylinders' on the centre of each plate. Top each cylinder with a tomato. Spoon the *shiso-ume* purée around the calamari and sprinkle it with chopped *shiso* leaves. Sprinkle the onion over the tomatoes. Garnish each plate with 3 *kaiware* stems.

DAIKON SALAD WITH KIWIFRUIT SAUCE

SERVES 4

300g (10oz) daikon

salt

4 leaves mitsuba *(trefoil)*

a handful of shredded nori

KIWIFRUIT SAUCE

2 kiwifruit, peeled and puréed

1 leaf mitsuba *(trefoil), whole*

½ teaspoon mirin

4 tablespoons rice vinegar

1 tablespoon castor sugar

1 tablespoon salt

Mitsuba *looks similar to Italian parsley, and its taste lies somewhere between parsley and celery. It is in season throughout autumn and winter. Coriander (cilantro) could be used as a substitute for* mitsuba *in this dish. Pre-shredded* nori *is available from Japanese and Asian grocery shops. Alternatively,* nori *can be cut into quarters with kitchen scissors and then cut thinly.*

Peel the *daikon* and rub in some salt. Trim off the ends to make a cylinder, then slice in half lengthwise and cut into 1cm (½in) dice.

To make the kiwifruit sauce, mix all ingredients together with a whisk.

Spoon the dressing onto the middle of serving plates. Place a little diced *daikon* on the side. Arrange the *mitsuba* leaf on top and sprinkle over the *nori*.

COLD PORK SALAD WITH PLUM DRESSING AND DAIKON

豚肉のミゾレ和え

SERVES 4

400g (14oz) pork fillet, thinly sliced
iced water
100g (3½oz) daikon, grated
2 pieces myōga, finely sliced
8 chives, finely chopped

PLUM DRESSING
½ cup (100g/3½oz) bainiku (plum purée)
1 tablespoon olive oil
1 teaspoon soy sauce

This is an ideal summer dish. Freeze the pork and cut with a sharp knife while semi-frozen to obtain thin slices. Myōga is available from Japanese food shops or good greengrocers during summer. If you can't find it, use a finely grated piece of ginger (about 5cm/2in long) instead.

Bring a pot of salted water to the boil. Blanch the pork slices one by one and chill in a bowl of iced water. Drain, then place the pork on a tray. Cover and refrigerate until ready to use.

To make the plum dressing, combine the *bainiku*, olive oil and soy sauce in a large bowl, and whisk until well combined. Place the cold pork slices on 4 serving plates. Arrange the *daikon*, topped with chopped chives and Myōga, beside the pork and place the dressing on the side, as pictured left.

COLD CHICKEN AND SEAWEED SALAD WITH SESAME-MISO DRESSING

鶏の胡麻味噌サラダ

SERVES 4

400g (14oz) chicken breast fillets
1 tablespoon mirin
1 tablespoon vegetable oil
80g (2¾oz) ugo (salted fresh seaweed)
¼ punnet mustard cress
12 preserved cranberries

SESAME-MISO DRESSING
2 tablespoons white sesame paste
3 tablespoons white miso
1 teaspoon roasted white sesame seeds
1 tablespoon rice vinegar
1 tablespoon vegetable oil
1 tablespoon mirin
2 tablespoons castor sugar
pinch of salt

Use a knife to score the surface of the chicken breasts. Sprinkle *mirin* over the chicken and leave on a tray for 10 minutes. Heat the oil in a frying pan. Add the chicken, and cook over medium heat, turning occasionally. When cooked, transfer to a tray and leave at room temperature until cool enough to handle. Flake the flesh into bite-sized pieces with fingers.

Rinse *ugo* under running water, then leave it in a bowl of water for 10 minutes. Drain well and transfer onto a board, then chop. Combine the chicken and *ugo* in a bowl and toss to mix. Refrigerate until needed.

To make the sesame-*miso* dressing, combine the sesame paste, *miso*, roasted sesame seeds and rice vinegar with a whisk. Add the vegetable oil, *mirin* and sugar, and mix. Add salt to taste.

Take the chicken out of the refrigerator and arrange on serving plates. Pour over the dressing. Arrange mustard cress and cranberries on each dish and serve.

サラダと香もの

NANOHANA WITH YUZU AND SHICHIMI SALAD

菜の花サラダ

If kanpyō *isn't available, kelp strips can be used (see page 29 'Lotus Root and Tomato with Sanshō Vinaigrette').*

SERVES 4

4 kanpyō (dried gourd) strings, each 10cm (4in) long
1 tablespoon salt
8 nanohana (canola) stems

YUZU DRESSING
1 tablespoon yuzu (Japanese citrus) flakes
½ teaspoon shichimi (Japanese seven-spice powder)
¼ cup (60ml/2fl oz) rice vinegar
1 tablespoon olive oil
1 teaspoon soy sauce
1 tablespoon mirin

Bring a pot of water to the boil and add the *kanpyō*. Cook for 10 minutes. Drain and set aside until ready to use.

Bring another pot of water to the boil, add the salt and blanch the *nanohana*. Drain, then leave under running water until cold. Drain again, then refrigerate until ready to use.

To make the *yuzu* dressing, combine the *yuzu, shichimi* and rice vinegar in a bowl with chopsticks or a fork. Add the oil, soy sauce and *mirin* and mix until well combined.

Take the *nanohana* out of the refrigerator and cut into 5cm (2in) lengths. Bundle each stem into a small parcel, with the leaves wrapped around the outside and the flower tops visible at one end. Bind each parcel with a *kanpyō* string to hold it firmly in place.

Arrange on a serving plate. Serve with the *yuzu* dressing on the side.

JAPANESE CABBAGE PICKLE WITH CHILLI

白菜の漬物

SERVES 4

This dish must be made at least one week in advance.

4 hakusai (Japanese cabbage) leaves
1 cup (250g/8oz) salt
½ cup (125ml/4fl oz) sake
1 teaspoon yuzu (Japanese citrus) powder
4 strips kombu (kelp), each 25cm (10in) long, wiped with a cloth
4 fresh red chillies, chopped
yuzu powder for serving
soy sauce

Rinse the *hakusai* leaves gently and drain. Leave them under shade on a bamboo basket or a cake rack for 2–3 hours until partially dry or until they begin to wilt, turning the leaves over a couple of times.

Sprinkle 3 pinches of salt into a container and neatly place the leaves in it, arranging them so that the stalk end of one meets the leaf end of another. Sprinkle over the remaining salt, the *sake* and the *yuzu*, then top with the *kombu* and chilli. Cover the container with plastic film or a lid and weigh down with a heavy stone or some cans. Leave for 5 days in a cool and dark place in winter, or in a refrigerator in summer. When water appears out of the *hakusai*, usually after about a month, it is time to serve.

Remove the *hakusai* and squeeze out the water with your hands. Trim the leaves into 3–4cm (1½in) lengths with a knife. Roll up 4 pieces into a bundle and tie with the *kombu* string. Top with a fresh chilli and sprinkle over some *yuzu* powder. Serve as pictured opposite, at far left. You could also serve a small dish of soy sauce on the side.

APRICOT WITH BAINIKU

杏子と梅の漬物

SERVES 4

4 dried apricots
1 tablespoon mirin
4 pinches katsuo-bushi (bonito flakes)
100g (3½ oz) bainiku (plum purée)
extra katsuo-bushi

Other dried fruits such as dried mangoes and dried papaya (pawpaw) can be used in this dish. Bainiku is puréed ume-boshi *without shiso and has a brighter red colour than shiso-ume. Bottled bainiku is available from Japanese grocery shops. You can also make bainiku by blending 3 pitted, medium-sized* ume-boshi *and then sieving the resulting purée.*

Bring a pan of water to the boil, add the apricots and cook until they swell and soften. Drain. Transfer the apricots into a bowl and drizzle over the *mirin*.

Sprinkle over the *katsuo-bushi* and add the *bainiku*. Combine with your hands. Cover the bowl with cling film and refrigerate overnight. Serve in bowls and top with *katsuo-bushi*, as pictured opposite, at right.

DESSERTS

Japanese desserts were once used to showcase seasonal fruits, dried fruits or steamed sweets made of sweet paste and rice flour.

Influences from other countries have brought about some changes in Japanese desserts. In the past, people hardly imagined that *matcha* (green tea) ice-cream would become one of the most popular Japanese desserts outside Japan. Despite this, Japanese desserts have kept many traditional ingredients and styles, such as sweet pastes made from beans or vegetables sweetened with sugar.

KAKI (PERSIMMON) JELLY

柿ゼリー

MAKES 4

The persimmon is an autumn fruit. If persimmon are not in season you could use ripe kiwifruit or blood plums as a substitute.

MILK JELLO
½ cup (125ml/4fl oz) whole milk
1 tablespoon gelatin powder
1 tablespoon castor sugar

To make milk jello, place milk and gelatin in a pan, and whisk for one minute. Bring to the boil then reduce the heat and simmer, stirring occasionally until the gelatin is dissolved. Add sugar, stir until sugar is dissolved, then remove from the heat. Pour the mixture into 4 dessert glasses and refrigerate.

KAKI JELLO
1 tablespoon gelatin powder
¼ cup (60ml/2fl oz) water
4 ripe small **kaki** *(persimmons)*
80g (2¾ oz) castor sugar
2 tablespoons sherry
4 **kaki** *(persimmon) leaves or 4 sprigs mint*

To make *kaki* jello, dissolve gelatin in water, peel *kaki*, cut into 4 pieces and remove the seeds. Purée the pieces in a blender or a food processor. Pass the purée through a fine sieve into a pan, and add the sugar and sherry. Simmer for a few minutes. Add the dissolved gelatin, mix well and remove from the heat.

Pour the *kaki* mixture over the milk jello and refrigerate until set.

Serve chilled with a *kaki* leaf or a sprig of mint.

NASHI AND KIWIFRUIT BAVAROIS

梨とキューイのババロア

SERVES 4

1 nashi
2 kiwifruit
½ cup (125ml/4fl oz) thick cream
5 egg yolks
100ml (3½ fl oz) whole milk
¼ cup (60g/2oz) castor sugar
1 teaspoon gelatin, soaked in a
teaspoon of water
4 sprigs mint

CARAMEL
½ cup (125ml/4fl oz) water
½ cup (120g/4oz) castor sugar

Peel and quarter the *nashi*. Cut out and discard the core. Place the quarters in a blender or a food processor and blend until smooth. Transfer to a bowl.

Peel the kiwifruit and blend in a food processor until smooth. Transfer to a bowl.

Whip the cream until soft peaks form. With a spatula, gently fold half the whipped cream into the *nashi* purée and the other half into the kiwifruit purée. Pass each purée through a sieve into separate bowls and refrigerate.

Beat the egg yolks in a large bowl. Combine the milk and sugar in a large heatproof bowl and mix well. Pour the beaten egg yolks into the milk and whisk together until well combined.

Bring a pot of water to the boil and place the bowl over the pot. Lower the heat to a gentle simmer and stir the mixture until warm and slightly thickened. Add the gelatin and stir until it is completely dissolved. When the mixture thickens, remove it from the heat and refrigerate until chilled.

Take the *nashi* and kiwifruit purées out of the refrigerator. Divide the egg mixture into 2 bowls. Add the *nashi* purée to one bowl and the kiwifruit purée to the other. Gently fold through with a spatula. Refrigerate until well chilled.

To make the caramel, bring water to the boil then add sugar and mix with a wooden spoon. Reduce heat and simmer gently, stirring occasionally, until sugar caramelises. Lay baking paper on a tray. Hold the wooden spoon over the paper and allow drops of caramel to fall onto the paper. Place the tray in the refrigerator for 10 minutes.

To serve, place a scoop of each bavarois into serving bowls or glasses, garnish with a mint leaf and place caramel drops around the inside edges of each dish.

MITSUMAME (FRUIT AND JAPANESE JELLY WITH SWEET RED BEANS IN SYRUP)

SERVES 4

1 cup (220g/7oz) red beans, rinsed and
soaked for 4–5 hours
2 tablespoons castor sugar
pinch of salt

SUGAR SYRUP
2 tablespoons castor sugar
1 tablespoon honey
1 cup (250ml/8fl oz) water

BLACK SYRUP
2 tablespoons brown sugar
1 tablespoon honey
2 tablespoons water

KANTEN JELLY
2 teaspoons kanten *(agar-agar) powder*
or 1 kanten *stick*
1 cup (250ml/8fl oz) water
½ cup (120g/4oz) sugar

FRUIT
2 fresh mandarines or 125g/4oz tinned
mandarine pieces
12 cherries, unstoned
½ cantaloupe (rockmelon), cut into
1cm (½in) cubes
8 strips canteloupe (rockmelon) peel,
(1cm x 10cm/ ½in x 4in) long, for garnish
4 sprigs mint, for garnish

To make the red beans, follow the directions on page 147.

To make the sugar syrup, combine the sugar, honey and water in a pan and bring to the boil, stirring until the sugar and honey dissolve. Chill in the refrigerator.

To make the black syrup, combine the brown sugar, honey and water in a pan and bring to the boil, stirring until the sugar and honey dissolve. Remove from the heat and refrigerate.

To make the *kanten* jelly, soak the powdered *kanten* in the water for 10 minutes before cooking. Do not drain. (If using a *kanten* stick, rinse and tear *kanten* into pieces and soak in a bowl of water for 1 hour. Drain and squeeze the *kanten* to remove excess water. Discard excess water and transfer sticks to a pan, then add 1 cup of water.)

Simmer the *kanten* and water mixture over a low heat until the *kanten* has dissolved, stirring occasionally. Add sugar and stir until dissolved. Remove from the heat, and pass through a fine sieve into a 10cm (4in) square tin. Refrigerate until set. When set, run a knife along the edges to loosen, and invert onto a board. Cut into 1cm (½in) cubes.

Arrange *kanten* cubes, fruit and red beans in chilled serving bowls. Knot 2 strips of canteloupe peel together at the centre points. Repeat with other pieces of peel. Arrange peel crosswise over each bowl. Pour over the syrups and serve.

MATCHA GLACÉ AND CHOCOLATE CHESTNUTS

愛の甘露煮抹茶風味チョコレート

Fresh chestnuts are widely available in autumn and frozen chestnuts are available all year round at Asian grocery shops.

If using fresh chestnuts, carefully make a small cut through each shell, taking care not to cut the kernel. Place in a pot of water. Discard any chestnuts that float. Bring to the boil and cook for 15 minutes. Test for tenderness with a skewer. When cooked, drain well and remove shells. Keep 4 shells intact for garnish. If using frozen chestnuts, defrost the chestnuts at room temperature, place them in a pan of boiling water and cook over medium heat for 15 minutes, then drain.

Transfer the chestnuts to a new pan, add the water and rock sugar, and simmer until the rock crystal sugar is melted. Do not stir, as the chestnuts damage easily.

SERVES 4

16 chestnuts, fresh or frozen
2 cups (500ml/16fl oz) water
½ cup (120g/4oz) rock crystal sugar
3 tablespoons matcha (green tea) powder
1 tablespoon mirin
2 tablespoons kuzu (starch), dissolved in
2 tablespoons water
100g (3½oz) white cooking chocolate
100g (3½oz) bitter dark cooking chocolate
2 cumquats, quartered

In a small bowl, combine the *matcha* and *mirin*. Add this mixture to the chestnuts and sugar, and simmer for another 10 minutes, gently stirring with a wooden spoon or a spatula until well combined. Take care not to break the chestnuts. Add the *kuzu* and simmer, gently stirring, until smooth, then take off the heat. Chill in the refrigerator for about 1 hour.

Refrigerate 4 plates until needed.

Break the white chocolate into small pieces and put in a small heatproof bowl. Prepare a bowl of hot water and place the bowl with the chocolate into the hot water. With a fork or a small spatula, stir until melted. Put 4 *matcha*-coated chestnuts into the melted white chocolate to coat and, with a fork, transfer them onto a tray covered with baking paper. Refrigerate until the chocolate sets.

Melt the dark chocolate in the same way in a separate bowl. Place 8 *matcha*-coated chestnuts into the melted dark chocolate to coat and transfer onto a tray covered with baking paper. On a separate tray covered with baking paper, use a teaspoon to make 4 abstract designs from the remaining dark chocolate. Place both trays in the refrigerator until the chocolates set.

To serve, place 1 white chocolate-coated chestnut, 2 dark chocolate-coated chestnuts, 1 *matcha*-coated chestnut and 1 chestnut shell on each plate. Gently place one abstract piece of dark chocolate vertically between the chestnuts on each plate. Garnish with cumquats and serve.

TEA

Since the fifteenth century, 'Teaism' or 'the art of tea' has been an integral part of Japanese culture. *O-cha* is a general term for all tea in Japanese ('o' being the honorific).

Cha or green tea is made from the leaves of the tea plant, and the same leaves are used in black tea. The leaves are steamed and dried for green tea, but fermented for black tea. Green tea is the most popular beverage among Japanese people, and it is customary for Japanese restaurants to serve green tea to customers before a meal.

Tea has been used in China for botanical and medicinal purposes since very early times. Its use as a beverage came later (around 800AD). The fifteenth century saw Japan enoble tea-drinking into a religion of aestheticism—*sadō*. 'Teaism' is a cult founded on the adoration of beauty among the banality of everyday existence through serving and drinking tea in a certain manner. The search for, and the understanding of, aestheticism in life is a continuing quest, and one that exerts great influence on Japanese culture. Powdered green tea (*matcha*), not tea leaves, is used in *sadō*. *Matcha* is considered 'the tea of teas' in Japan.

Because green tea was first and foremost a medicinal plant, it is not only delicious, but contains great quantities of vitamins, minerals and polyphenols. Polyphenols are powerful antioxidants that have been shown to fight viruses, slow the ageing process, and have a generally beneficial effect on health. Japanese green tea has an individual taste, aroma and style that is completely different from Chinese green tea.

There are about seven varieties of Japanese green tea: *ryokucha, gyokuro, matcha, sencha, hōjicha, bancha* and *genmaicha*. The particular blend depends on the part of the leaves used, the processing technique and what the leaves are blended with.

Keep green tea in an airtight tin or caddy to prevent any exposure to sunlight, and store the tin in a dry area. It is better to finish a package of tea within a month of opening, as tea loses its taste and aroma when it comes into contact with air. It is sometimes hard to get fresh green tea outside Japan, so check the date of packaging before you purchase.

Besides green tea, Chinese herbal teas, flower teas, Japanese herbal teas, European herbal teas and *kombu-cha* (powdered kelp tea) are also enjoyed in Japan. Japanese green tea is drunk without milk or sugar.

日本茶の種類と説明

BREWING

Pour some hot water into the teapot (*kyūsu*) and leave for a couple of minutes until the vessel is warm. Empty the pot, add the required amount of tea leaves and hot water. Still mineral or spring water is preferable to tap water for brewing tea. (Tap water may contain chemicals that affect the taste.) The water temperature and the brewing time depend on the kind of tea, while the right amount of tea can vary according to the individual, so taste, experiment and adjust the proportions to your liking. Serve the tea in individual cups (*yunomi*) which have no handles.

TYPES OF JAPANESE TEA

RYOKUCHA (GREEN TEA)

Ryokucha is a general term for 'green tea' or 'Japanese tea'. Only young green leaves are used for *ryokucha*. The leaves are picked, steamed, dried and ground into brownish-green tea.

MATCHA (GREEN TEA POWDER)

To produce *matcha*, the leaves are steamed and dried, the stems discarded, and the leaves ground with a stone mortar to make a powder.

Matcha is used for tea ceremonies. You cannot use green tea powder like powdered coffee—the powder needs to be stirred or 'whipped' with a bamboo whisk. Due to the complex, traditional, time-consuming rituals associated with drinking *matcha*, many Japanese people consider it too complicated to prepare and enjoy every day. Today, however, drinking *matcha* does not have to be so complicated, and the following somewhat abbreviated method allows this relaxing ceremony to be incorporated into busy daily life.

To make weak green tea, put ½ teaspoon of green tea powder into a tea bowl and add ½ cup (125ml/4fl oz) of hot water. Using a bamboo tea whisk, place the tip of the handle against your palm and, keeping the whisk vertically upright in the bowl, whisk vigorously until fine bubbles cover the surface of the tea.

GYOKURO

Gyokuro is the most superior grade of green tea. It has a sweet flavour within the bitterness. The producers of *gyokuro* choose leaves that come from bushes that are more than ten years old. About two weeks before picking they cover the trees to protect the leaves from direct sunlight, then pick only young leaves. They steam the leaves for a short time, dry them, then leave them for a couple of months to enhance the flavour. Japanese people consider it a luxurious beverage, as it uses only the best leaves and is produced with superb care.

To prepare *gyokuro*, allow 1 teaspoonful of tea leaves per person and steep for 3–4 minutes before serving. The tea should be brownish-green in colour. The optimum temperature for drinking *gyokuro* is 60°C (130°F).

SENCHA

To produce *sencha*, tea leaves are steamed and then lightly ground. *Sencha* has a light aroma and less sweetness and bitterness than other green teas.

To prepare *sencha*, warm the teapot and cups. Place 1 heaped tablespoon of tea into the pot, then pour over some boiling water. Steep for 30–40 seconds, then pour into cups. First-poured tea is aromatic, the second has more sweetness, and the third can be enjoyed for its bitterness. *Sencha* is the most commonly available green tea.

BANCHA

Bancha is the most economical form of green tea. It is produced from the discarded rough leaves left over from making *gyokuro*. *Bancha* is less bitter than other green teas.

To prepare *bancha*, bring water to the boil and pour into a warmed teapot with 2 level tablespoons of tea leaves. Serve and drink immediately.

HŌJICHA

Hōjicha is produced by roasting *bancha* tea leaves over a high heat. This imparts a delicate, roasted fragrance. *Hōjicha* contains less tannin and caffeine than *bancha*.

To prepare *hōjicha*, place 2 level tablespoons of tea in a warmed teapot and add boiling water. Steep for 10 seconds before pouring and serving.

GENMAICHA

To produce *genmaicha*, *Hōjicha* is mixed with roasted rice grains, imparting a nutty flavour to the tea.

To prepare *genmaicha* place 2 level tablespoons of tea in a warmed teapot, add hot water and steep for 2 minutes before pouring and serving.

OTHER TEAS

MUGICHA (BARLEY TEA)

Mugicha originated in Japan around the third century, and was the most common beverage in Japan before green tea was introduced from the Asian continent. Nowadays, cold *mugicha* is still popular as a summer refreshment.

To prepare *mugicha*, bring 1 litre of water to the boil, add 3 tablespoons of roasted barley and leave for 10 minutes. Strain then discard the barley and pour the liquid into a glass bottle. Cool the liquid to room temperature then refrigerate. Bottled *mugicha* will keep for a couple of days when stored this way.

THE JAPANESE KITCHEN

Each Japanese kitchen has a different story and character, depending on the traditions that were handed down through the family that uses it, and the cooks who have used it.

Today, most Japanese kitchens do not differ greatly from the average western kitchen. Japanese kitchens usually contain some utensils, tableware and ingredients that would be familiar to many western cooks. However, many unique utensils and ingredients would also be found in addition to these, including the *sudare* (*sushi* mat), distinctive tableware, and unfamiliar ingredients, all of which are an important part of daily life in Japan.

日本の厨房

HŌCHŌ (JAPANESE KNIVES)

Knives are mainly divided into two types: double-edged (western-type) blades and single-edged (Japanese-type) blades (including Japanese Samurai swords). A Japanese knife has a single-edged blade with a very delicate tip, and gives a sharper result than a double-edged one. However, a Japanese knife needs more honing, as it loses its edge and gets rusty quite easily.

Professional Japanese chefs use a wide variety of knives. For cooking at home two or three types of Japanese knifes are sufficient. Pictured left (from left to right) are the *yanagiba-bōchō* (*sashimi* slicing knife), the *usuba-bōchō* (vegetable knife) and the *deba-bōchō* (filleting knife).

OROSHIGANE (GRATER)

A Japanese grater can be made of copper, plastic, aluminium, stainless steel or ceramic, and will have tiny dense edges on the surface. When using such a grater, especially when grating ginger and *wasabi*, move your hand in a circular motion.

SLICER OR MANDOLIN

Mandolin slicers do the work more rapidly and accurately than knives. The mandolin has several blades, which are used for cutting julienne strips or slices of different sizes and thicknesses. Japanese cooks also use a spin slicer to reduce vegetables to hair-like shreds. When purchasing a slicer, choose one designed for safety.

SUDARE OR MAKISU (SUSHI MAT)

The *sudare* is a small mat made of narrow strips of bamboo, and it is vital for rolling *sushi*. Several sizes of *sudare* are available, from those that are wider than a whole *nori* sheet to small ones to those made of thicker bamboo strips that are used to shape rolled omelettes. After use, brush the mat thoroughly with a sponge and dry in bright sunlight. The larger mats are more versatile.

SAIBASHI (LONG CHOPSTICKS)

Saibashi are a pair of long chopsticks made of bamboo. Their length makes them ideal for use when deep-frying or for stirring hot dishes.

RICE COOKER

Rice used to be cooked in a heavy pot with a tight-fitting lid, but nowadays automatic electric or gas rice cookers are commonplace and do a wonderful job. Electric rice cookers with a keep-warm feature are also available.

日本の厨房

Uroko-tori (Fish scaler)

The Japanese scaler (pictured left) has a thicker and rounder top than the western type, and is designed to cause less damage to the surface of the fish. To use the *uroko-tori*, draw it over the body of a fish, from tail to head, against the grain of the scales.

Hone-nuki (Tweezers)

Japanese tweezers have wide, flat tips designed to efficiently remove fish bones.

Suribachi and Surikogi (Mortar and Pestle)

An earthenware bowl with a wooden pestle that is used to pulverise ingredients such as sesame seeds. A feature of the Japanese grinding bowl is the inside surface, which has fine, sharp ridges to hold the seeds against the pestle. *Suribachi* are available in several sizes, but one about 20cm (8in) in diameter is sufficient for most grinding. A blender can also be used.

Hangiri (Sushi Bowl)

This wide, flat-bottomed wooden vessel is used for combining cooked rice with a vinegar mixture to make *sushi* rice. The wood absorbs excess moisture and the large surface area allows the rice to cool rapidly, which gives it a glossy sheen. A large wooden salad bowl can be substituted. To make enough rice to serve three or four people, a tub about 50cm (20in) in diameter is required. Before using, wipe the inside thoroughly with a cloth dipped in a mixture of vinegar and water to prevent the rice sticking to the inside.

Hibachi (Charcoal Burner)

In Japan, the *hibachi* was the main source of winter heating before gas and kerosene heaters came into general use. It was also the main device for cooking, especially for stewing. The *hibachi* can be made of wood, bronze, iron, brass, copper or porcelain. Recently, *hibachi* have assumed a more decorative role at the table. When purchasing, check that the *hibachi* you buy can be used as a practical utensil.

Katanuki (Vegetable Cutters)

Many varieties of vegetable cutters are available in Japan, including those pictured on page 56. Specialty kitchenware shops may also carry a range of cutters. If unavailable, use metal cookie cutters instead. Slice the vegetable thinly first. Place the slices on a wooden board (harder surfaces could damage the edge of the cutters), and push the cutter through to cut out a shape. The type of vegetables you can use depends on the size of the cutters.

日本の厨房

A distinguishing feature of Japanese cuisine is the beauty of the tableware itself. Japanese people love the warmth of wood, and cherish its pleasant feel against the skin and its comfortable weight in the hands. The hard, cold chill of metal is not congenial to the traditional Japanese way of eating with bowl in one hand and chopsticks in the other, even though metal bowls were introduced to Japan as early as the eighth century.

Increasing industrialisation in the Meiji and Tasihō periods (1867–1925) affected the manufacture of porcelain and glass, making mass-produced, cheap wares available to all. Traditional lacquerware, impossible to mass produce, was priced out of competition and slowly faded from the market. Nowadays, there is keen interest in traditional, quality Japanese kitchenware.

BOWLS

Bowls are made of lacquer, urethane, ceramic, china, glass, wood or bamboo. They are used for soups, rice, dipping sauces, dishes or desserts.

PLATES

Japanese plates are usually ceramic, china, lacquer, urethane or glass. They are designed for serving several dishes together.

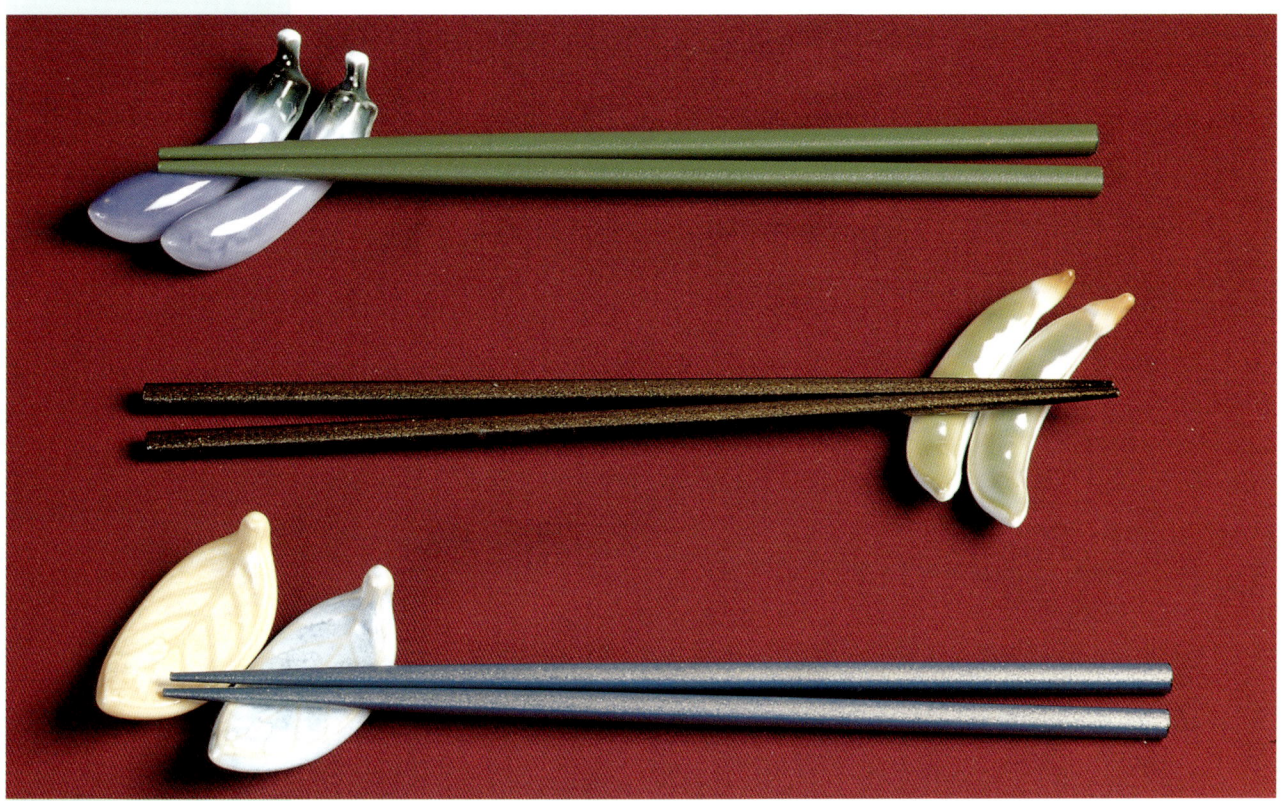

CHOPSTICKS AND CHOPSTICK PILLOWS

Japanese chopsticks (*hashi*) are made of many different materials and also come in a variety of sizes. The sizes may depend on the diner's age and gender, and on the formality of the occasion. There are some specialised chopsticks such as those with a 'stopper' to use when eating slippery food or with a device to allow for easier eating. Disposable chopsticks, usually made of wood or bamboo waste, are used at many restaurants. Chopstick pillows are small, attractive pieces of porcelain that diners use to rest their chopsticks on when they are not in use. Small pebbles or shells can also work well.

TEAPOTS AND TEACUPS

Teapots (*kyūsa*) for brewing tea come in a huge range of sizes, shapes and materials. Most teapots are ceramic or porcelain, though nowadays even glass and aluminium may be used. Many teapots are designed to retain tea leaves inside the teapot when the tea is being poured into cups. Japanese teacups (*yunomi*) do not have handles.

日本の厨房

INGREDIENTS

GROCERIES

AONORI (GREEN SEAWEED FLAKES)

Aonori is dried seaweed, flaked into small pieces. It is sold in packets or jars at Asian or Japanese food stores. It is sprinkled over food just before serving. Choose dark green flakes.

JAPANESE AZUKI (ADZUKI OR RED BEANS)

Several types of small red beans are used in Japanese desserts. They are also available in glaze form (*amanatto*) or in a paste. Japanese sweet cakes and confectionery mostly use a sweet *azuki* (red bean) paste as a filling. These cakes contain sweetness with less fat and protein than the many desserts throughout the western world, which rely on animal fats including butter and eggs.

BAINIKU (UME-BOSHI PURÉE)

Bainiku is a purée of *ume-boshi* (Japanese pickled plum). It is used as a topping and a dip, or in dressings. It is available from Japanese food shops in a bottle or a tube.

DŌMYŌJI-KO (STEAMED AND ROASTED STICKY RICE)

Used in Japanese desserts, *dōmyōji-ko* is readily available at Japanese grocery shops.

GARI (SLICED GINGER IN VINEGAR)

A condiment served with *sushi*. To make *gari*, young ginger is peeled, sliced thinly, blanched and pickled in a sweet vinegar.

GOMA (SESAME SEEDS)

Nutty-flavoured, oil-rich little black or white seeds that are used roasted or unroasted in Japanese cooking. Seeds are sprinkled over the finished dish or ground into sauces and dressings. Ground sesame paste (*goma dare*) is available in tubes. Sesame salt (*goma shio*) is a mixture of well-ground sesame seeds and salt, used as a condiment.

HŌBA (*FICUS LYRATA* LEAF)

An inedible leaf, used dried to wrap beef or fish before cooking. The leaf imparts a strong aroma to meat when cooked on the *hibachi* (a small charcoal burner). Cut fresh leaves into approximately 15cm x 30cm (6in x 12in) pieces and dry in the shade. It is best to buy the whole plant from a nursery and cultivate the plant to harvest the leaves as you need them.

KANPYŌ (DRIED GOURD SHAVINGS)

Kanpyō is made from the cream-coloured flesh of the white-flowered gourd (*yūgao*). The pith is shaved into very long, thin strips and dried. It is used as a filling in *sushi* rolls and also in soups, and as an edible tie or string for food. It is sold in packets in Japanese food shops.

日本の厨房

KANTEN (AGAR-AGAR)

A gelatin-like substance that is used as a setting agent. It is made from several varieties of red seaweed and melts at a higher temperature than gelatin, and so is more useful in hot weather. Agar-agar is sold in strands (as pictured on page 82) or as a powder in Asian food shops.

KATAKURIKO (POTATO STARCH)

Katakuriko is a special potato starch. It is sold in packets in Japanese food shops and is used to thicken soups or sauces, and added to tempura flour to give a crispy result.

KATSUO-BUSHI (DRIED BONITO FLAKES)

The bonito is a member of the mackerel family. Dried bonito fillets are shaved into translucent flakes to be sprinkled on food just before serving (see picture page 38). Along with *kombu* (kelp), *katsuo-bushi* is an indispensable ingredient in *dashi*, the basic Japanese soup stock. Dried bonito flakes are sold in packets in Asian and Japanese food shops.

KOMBU (DRIED KELP)

Kombu (or *konbu*) is rich in glutamic acid, calcium, iodine and iron. It is one of the basic ingredients of Japanese stocks used in Japanese cooking. After wiping *kombu* with a wet cloth, add to boiling water to make a *kombu* stock. It can also be deep-fried. *Kombu* is sold in packets in Asian and Japanese food shops. Keep in an airtight container once the packet has been opened.

KOME (JAPONICA SHORT-GRAIN RICE)

Japonica short-grain rice has a more rounded shape than long-grain rice varieties such as jasmine rice. When Japonica rice is cooked with water, it becomes slightly gluey in texture and the grains cling together. This is ideal for Japanese cuisine.

KOMEZU (RICE VINEGAR)

Komezu is suitable for Japanese cuisine, especially for making *sushi* rice. It tastes a little like white vinegar, but it has a thicker consistency. White vinegar is a suitable substitute, but it is worth finding the real thing if possible.

KUZU (KUZU STARCH)

A high-quality thickener made from the *kuzu* potato. It is similar to *katakuriko*, but once *kuzu* has melted and set, it keeps its shape, unlike *katakuriko*. It is used to thicken soups or stews, and in desserts or dumplings as a wrapper. It is available from Japanese grocery shops.

MIDORI (JAPANESE LIQUEUR)

A Japanese liqueur flavoured with honeydew melon. It has a distinctive intense emerald green colour. *Midori* is quite sweet, so it is good as an apéritif or a digestif.

日本の厨房

Mirin (Sweet Cooking Rice Wine)

Mirin gives a glossy appearance and a slightly sweet taste to food. When grilling, brush *mirin* over an ingredient for a nice golden colour. When stewing, add a little *mirin* to enhance the taste.

Miso (Fermented Soybean Paste)

Miso is a very flavoursome ingredient. 'White' and 'red' varieties are available, but the colour may range from dark brown to creamy gold. (The colour depends on the length of fermentation.) The lighter varieties tend to be less salty and sweeter than the darker varieties. White *miso* is more popular for soups, sauces and seasoning.

Nori (Roasted Seaweed Sheet)

Nori is used to make *sushi* rolls. It is usually sold toasted or untoasted, in a cellophane or plastic bag. Once opened, store in an air-tight container or use straight away. If you purchase untoasted *nori*, lightly toast each sheet over an open flame before using.

Sake (Japanese Rice Wine)

Sake is made from fermented rice that is brewed and matured. It has a huge range of flavours and can be dry or sweet. *Sake* can be served either hot or cold, depending on the season and the style of *sake*. Naturally, cooking *sake* is cheaper than drinking *sake*, and the two are not really interchangeable, but if you have left-over *sake*, it can be used for cooking. When used in cooking, a small amount of *sake* enhances the flavour of other ingredients.

Sanshō (Japanese Pepper Tree)

The leaves and berries of the *sanshō* tree are used in Japanese cooking. Dried and finely ground *sanshō* berries have a fragrant aroma and a sharp taste that is used in cooked dishes such as barbecued eel. The fresh leaves are used in clear Japanese soups and salads. *Sanshō* pepper is sold in small bottles in Japanese food stores.

Shichimi (Japanese Seven-spice Powder)

A blend of seven spices or herbs including chilli, Japanese pepper, rapeseed, citrus zest and other ingredients that vary depending on the spice seller. It is served with sauces or noodles.

Shītake Mushrooms

These are available fresh or dried, but only extra-fresh *shītake* can be eaten raw. Dried ones need to be soaked and cooked in one of the Japanese stocks (see page 145). Dried *shītake* contains more vitamins and aroma than the fresh. Leave them in strong sunlight for 30 minutes before soaking, as this will concentrate the flavour.

Shōyu (Japanese Soy Sauce)

Made from a fermented mixture of brine, wheat, malt and soybeans, Japanese soy sauce is slightly different from Chinese soy sauce. There are three types of soy sauce: *koi-kuchi* (dark soy), *usu-kuchi* (light soy), which is saltier, and others designed for particular dishes. For *sashimi*, use either *koi-kuchi*, *tamari* (thickened soy sauce) or *sashimi-jyōyu* (sashimi soy sauce).

Takuan (Pickled Daikon)

Pickled *daikon* comes in two colours, white or yellow, and can be sweet or salty. After drying the *daikon* under sunlight, it is pickled in salt and turmeric is added to colour it a bright yellow. The texture is crunchy and the taste is pungent. It is available in a plastic packets at Asian food shops.

Tōfu (Beancurd)

Two main kinds of *tōfu* are used: *momen-dōfu*, which has a firm texture, and *kinugoshi-dōfu*, which has a much finer and softer texture. *Momen-dōfu* is good for cooking, as it won't fall apart easily. *Kinugoshi-dōfu* is eaten raw in summer or as *yudō-fu*, which is *tōfu* cooked in boiling water in a flat-bottomed pot and served with a dipping sauce. Check the date on the packet and choose the freshest one from the refrigerated section of your Asian supermarket.

Ugo (Seaweed)

An edible red or green thin seaweed, usually sold salted in a packet. Before using *ugo*, it should be rinsed under running water to remove excess salt, and squeezed dry. *Ugo* is served with *sashimi* or salad.

Ume-boshi with Shiso (Dried, Salted Pickled Japanese Plum with Shiso)

The Japanese plum *ume-boshi* can be large or small, hard or soft. It is usually pickled with salt and coloured red by being preserved in red *shiso* leaves in a dark place for almost a year. It tastes much too salty to eat a whole large one, but it is good when combined with other ingredients and is used in pastes, dressings and sauces. The paste of *ume-shiso* purée (*shiso-ume*) is available from Japanese food shops in tubes or bottles.

Wasabi (Japanese Horseradish)

Wasabi powder and paste are well known, because they are convenient and inexpensive. The recipes in this book use *wasabi* paste sold in tubes. Fresh *wasabi* (as pictured on page 90) may be available at specialist grocers. It has a great texture and aroma and an extremely hot taste.

Yukari (Salted Red Shiso)

The rough-grained, dried red leaves of *shiso* (prickly ash) can be preserved in salt, resulting in a salty, sour condiment. It is popular in Japanese cuisine, sprinkled on rice or salads. It is sold in packets or bottles at Asian grocery shops.

Yuzu (Japanese Citron)

Only the zest or juice of *yuzu* is used as a condiment. The fresh zest can be sliced or grated into soups, sauces or salads. It has a delicate citrus aroma in winter. The juice is more sour than sweet, and is ideal in dressings and in combination with other ingredients. If not available fresh, dried or frozen *yuzu* is available from Japanese grocery stores.

Yuzu Miso

A combination of miso and grated *yuzu* zest, *yuzu miso* is used to thicken sauces. It is available in packets from Japanese grocery stores.

VEGETABLES AND FRUITS

BENISHOGA

Benishoga is young ginger that is salted and pickled in vinegar with red shiso or artificial colouring. It is sold sliced or shredded and is often used as a garnish. *Benishoga* is saltier than *gari*, the pickled pink ginger often served with *sushi*.

DAIKON (GIANT WHITE RADISH)

Daikon is used in stews, salads, as a condiment or pickle, and raw in sliced, grated or carved forms. Select *daikon* that has dense, tight flesh and no surface wrinkles (it has a milder flavour).

ENOKI MUSHROOMS

These creamy-coloured mushrooms have long, thin stems and tiny caps (as pictured top left). Wrapped in paper and refrigerated, they will keep well for a couple of days.

HAKUSAI (CHINESE CABBAGE)

One of the many varieties of Chinese cabbage, *hakusai* has a very high water content. It is often used in Japanese salads, pickles and stews.

KAKI (PERSIMMON)

There are two varieties of this autumn fruit. One type can be eaten raw, straight from the tree, and the other type needs to ripen after being harvested. The most readily available, orange-coloured persimmon can be eaten when the flesh is soft and the colour intensely orange.

KAIWARE (RADISH SPROUTS)

The taste of *kaiware* is similar to mustard cress, but the sprouts are longer (about 15cm/6in). Choose sprouts with crispy stems. They are used in salads and as a garnish.

KINOME (PRICKLY ASH LEAVES)

The young leaves of *sanshō* (prickly ash tree) pictured left, second from top, are used as a garnish. They can also be braised or made into a paste to impart a unique aromatic flavour.

KURI (CHESTNUTS)

Chestnuts are in season in autumn, when they can be consumed raw. Frozen or bottled chestnuts can also be used, but dried chestnuts are not suitable for Japanese cooking.

KYŪRI (CUCUMBER)

Japanese cucumbers are less watery than English cucumbers and measure about 20cm (8in) long. Lebanese cucumbers are similar to the Japanese variety and can be substituted.

MITSUBA (TREFOIL)

With a taste somewhere between celery and parsley, *mitsuba* (pictured left, third from top) is used in soups, *sushi*, salads and for garnish. Choose small leaves with a softer texture.

日本の厨房

Myōga (Myōga Ginger)

Myōga is in season from late spring to summer. Only buds and stems are eaten. Unlike the root, it is not hot. It is used in salads, *sushi*, soups, *sashimi* or as a garnish. (Pictured opposite page at bottom.)

Nanohana (Canola or Rape)

The edible yellow flowers of *nanohana* are produced in spring and are a popular garnish. The stems, leaves and flowers are used in salads, *tempura* and pickles.

Nashi (Chinese Pear or Apple Pear)

Unlike regular pears, *nashi* are low in acid and aroma and are quite hard even when ripe. They are rounded like an apple, and much crunchier and juicier than regular pears.

Renkon (Lotus Root)

Renkon is a rhizome with a crisp texture. A decorative pattern is revealed when it is sliced (pictured left at top). Peel, slice and boil them in water with a few drops of vinegar to keep the white colour. Fresh *renkon* is preferable to the frozen, canned or dried varieties.

Satoimo (Taro)

Unlike the common potato, *satoimo* has a hairy brown skin and a slimy texture that remains after cooking. Small *satoimo* weighing less than 100g (3½ oz) each are best. They are used in stews or soups. They are sometimes labelled as a type of yam.

Shimeji Mushrooms

Shimeji mushrooms (pictured left, second from top), have a delightful taste but only a mild aroma. The fat caps and stems are used in soups, grills and *tempura*.

Shiso

Shiso (pictured left, third from top), is readily available in summer, in green and red varieties. Red *shiso* leaves are used mostly to give colour to pickles, especially *ume-boshi* (pickled plum). Green *shiso* is used as a garnish in salads, *sashimi* or *sushi* for its distinctive aroma.

Shungiku (Garland or Spring Chrysanthemum)

The leaves of *shungiku* have a strong aroma and a distinctive flavour, and are used as a vegetable in hotpots and *tempura*, and fresh or blanched in a salad.

Takenoko (Bamboo Shoots)

Takenoko are used in stews, *tempura* or soups and are available in spring. Remove the husks and cook until soft. (Soak large shoots in water overnight with a teaspoonful of baking soda first.) Pre-cooked bamboo shoots are also available in vacuum packs.

Wasabi (Japanese Horseradish)

Fresh *wasabi* (pictured left, at bottom), has lovely texture and aroma, and an extremely hot taste. It is superior to the powders and pastes sold pre-made, but is not readily available outside Japan.

日本の厨房

FISH AND SEAFOOD

CALAMARI

This is the most suitable type of seafood for *sashimi*. It is more expensive than squid, but the flesh is chunky, delicious and has a sweet flavour. Choose calamari with a glossy, firm, undamaged skin. For instructions on how to clean calamari, see page 150.

CUTTLEFISH

Cuttlefish is available all year round from good fishmongers. Choose firm flesh with a mildly fishy smell. Avoid buying cuttlefish with a pinkish flesh. For instructions on how to clean cuttlefish, see page 150. Squid can be substituted for cuttlefish, but it must be extremely fresh.

GARFISH

Garfish with a short beak live in rivers; those with a longer beak live in the ocean. Both are suitable for *sashimi* or grilling. Ocean garfish have a beautiful appearance, with a long, slender body.

KING PRAWN (GIANT SHRIMP)

King prawns are very versatile and can be used in many types of Japanese dishes. They range in size from 10cm (4in) to 20cm (8in). Fresh (green) king prawns are used in *tempura,* while pre-cooked king prawns are suitable for use in general cooking and *sushi*. Look for plump, fresh, moist prawns with glossy shells and no black spots.

LOBSTER

For *sashimi*, choose a live lobster. The larger ones have firmer flesh and are less tasty. Choose one that weighs less than 600g (20oz), which will have soft flesh with more *umami* (deliciousness) and sweetness.

MAGURO (TUNA)

Tuna meat is usually sold in blocks. Choose flesh that is bright red in colour with clean-cut edges. In hot weather, yellowfin tuna is popular because it has less oil. In cold weather, bluefin and blackfin are popular because they are rich in fat.

SALMON

To choose fresh salmon, make sure the surface of the skin has a fresh layer of slime on it. The eyes should be glossy and the flesh should be firm and resilient when poked with a finger. Above all, it should smell fresh. Most salmon is sold cleaned. When purchasing a fillet, choose one with moist, firm, bright-coloured flesh.

日本の厨房

SQUID

Squid has a shorter shelf-life than calamari and cuttlefish. Only extra-fresh squid is suitable for sashimi. Squid can be grilled or deep-fried. For instructions on how to clean squid, see page 150.

UNAGI (JAPANESE EEL)

Unagi belong to the short blackfin eel family. For the purpose of grilling, choose an eel that weighs about 800g (1¾lb) gross/undressed weight. Larger eels are difficult to fillet and the skin becomes tough when grilled. If you cannot find fresh eel, you can purchase pre-grilled *teriyaki* eel in vacuum packs from Japanese grocery shops.

UNI (SEA URCHIN)

Sea urchins have a distinctive texture and deep flavour. You can purchase sea urchins in or off the shell. When buying out of the shell, choose flesh that is firm and bright orange in colour. When buying urchins still in the shell, you can check for freshness by touching the spikes—if it is very fresh the spikes will move.

PURCHASING FISH FOR SASHIMI

Always tell the fishmonger if you intend to use the fish or seafood for *sashimi*. The surest way to purchase fish and seafood fresh enough for *sashimi* is to find a reliable fishmonger and cultivate a rapport with him or her over time. You should always use your five senses too. Here are some hints:

Whole fish—The eyes must be bright and glossy, and the gills should be bright red. If the fish still has its guts, check its belly. If the belly looks brownish from the outside, the fish should be avoided. If the fish has been cleaned and gutted, it should be an appealing, bright colour inside—avoid it if the belly is pale.

Fish fillet—Tuna flesh should have a bright reddish tinge to the flesh, while salmon should be a bright orange colour. Avoid any *sashimi* fillets that are dry, overly slimy, pale or have a bad smell.

Cuttlefish—Bright, glossy flesh is a good indication of freshness. Never purchase cuttlefish for *sashimi* if they have black spots or a pink colour on the surface, and naturally, avoid any that have a bad smell.

Prawns—Shells should be bright and glossy. Definitely avoid any prawns that have black spots on the surface or a bad smell. For *sashimi*, you need to be very sure that the prawns are so fresh they are almost alive.

BASICS

The important basic steps and methods included in this section are
a little time-consuming, but they are the vital foundation of many of
the wonderful, complex flavours and visual beauty of Japanese food.

DASHI (STOCK)

Dashi is Japan's fundamental stock and seasoning, much used in Japanese cooking as a base and for soup. When well made, *dashi* has a wonderful aroma and goes particularly well with Japanese clear soup (*suimono*). The dipping sauce for tempura is based on stock made with *dashi*.

Katsuo-bushi (dried bonito flakes), *kombu* (kelp) and *shītake* mushrooms are used for *dashi*. Other ingredients, such as small dried prawns (shrimps), small fish (for example, dried anchovies) or fish or chicken bones are also sometimes used. The use of *kombu dashi* and *shītake dashi* indicates ancient Buddhist influences, which preclude the use of animal parts in cooking.

Dashi is known to contain *umami* (deliciousness), a feature much prized in Japanese cooking. *Umami* is a Japanese word meaning 'savoury', 'deliciousness', 'rich' or 'the scale of deliciousness that measures the taste of glutamate'. *Umami* was identified in 1908 by Kikunae Ikeda as the fifth primary taste after sweetness, bitterness, saltiness and sourness. Mrs Ikeda discovered that the glutamic acid in kelp stock emphasised the deliciousness of other ingredients. In the west it is known as monosodium glutamate, which is used as a flavour enhancer in cooking.

To make *dashi*, dried bonito flakes, kelp or *shītake* mushrooms are placed in boiling water and simmered very gently to extract the full true flavour of the base ingredient. The stock is then sieved, and used according to the recipe.

KATSUO (BONITO) DASHI

Freshly shaved dried bonito (katsuo-bushi) is used to make this standard stock for soups and sauces. The 'first' Katsuo Dashi has an incomparable aroma and is often used in clear soups and miso *soups. The second* dashi *has a weaker flavour and is often used in stews, or combined with other stocks. The dipping sauce for* tempura *also uses Katsuo Dashi.*

MAKES 4 CUPS (1 LITRE/2 PINTS)

8 cups (2 litres/4 pints) water
50g (1¾oz) katsuo-bushi (dried bonito) shavings

To make the first *Katsuo Dashi*, bring 4 cups (1 litre/2 pints) of water to the boil and add the *katsuo-bushi* shavings. When the *katsuo-bushi* shavings float to the surface, remove from heat. Drain the *Katsuo Dashi* into a pot. Set aside. Keep the *katsuo-bushi* shavings for the second stock. To make the second *Katsuo Dashi*, use the leftover shavings from the first *dashi* and repeat with another 4 cups (1 litre/2 pints) of water. Keep the stocks separate. Depending on the dish you intend to make, use one stock and keep the other refrigerated in a ceramic or glass bottle (it will only keep for a couple of days).

KOMBU (KELP) DASHI

Though less fragrant than Katsuo Dashi, Kombu Dashi *contributes greatly as a flavour enhancer because of the very high amount of natural monosodium glutamate it contains. It is used in almost all Japanese food, often in combination with bonito stock.* Kombu Dashi *is especially well suited to shellfish.*

MAKES 4 CUPS (1LITRE/2PINTS)

50g (1¾oz) kombu *(kelp)*
4 cups (1 litre/2 pints) water

Wipe the *kombu* lightly with a dry kitchen towel. Combine the *kombu* and water and bring to boil. When the water boils, remove the pan from the heat, and remove the *kombu* from the stock.

SHĪTAKE MUSHROOM DASHI

This flavoursome stock is used in stews or soups and is particularly useful for cooking vegetarian dishes.

MAKES 4 CUPS (1 LITRE/2 PINTS)

12 dried shītake *mushrooms*
4 cups (1 litre/2 pints) cold water

Place *shītake* mushrooms and cold water in a saucepan. Soak for 30 minutes, then bring to the boil. When the water boils, remove the pan from the heat and strain. Use the liquid as stock and retain the mushrooms for use in another dish.

SEASONED DASHI

You can combine one type of dashi *with another and add seasonings to impart extra flavour to stews and other dishes. Seasoned/mixed dashi can be made ahead of time and stored in the refrigerator for up to 2 days.*

MAKES 2 CUPS (500ML/16FL OZ)

1 cup (250ml/8fl oz) Katsuo Dashi *(see opposite)*
1 cup (250ml/8fl oz) Kombu Dashi *(see this page)*
1 tablespoon soy sauce
1 tablespoon mirin

Combine *Katsuo Dashi* and *Kombu Dashi* in a saucepan and simmer gently until warm. Do not boil. Add the soy sauce and *mirin*, mix well and remove the pan from the heat.

OTHER BASIC RECIPES

SUSHI RICE

MAKES 6 CUPS

3 cups (700g/1½ lbs) short-grain rice
3 cups (750ml/24fl oz) water

VINEGAR MIXTURE
½ cup (125ml/4fl oz) rice vinegar
¼ cup (60g/2oz) castor sugar
a pinch of salt

Place the rice in a bowl and pour some cool water into the bowl to wash the rice. Tip the water out. Pour fresh water until it just covers the rice. Wash the rice by pressing hard against it with your palm, but not so hard that you crush the grains. Pour away the water, mixing the rice with your fingers as you do so. Repeat this washing action three more times.

Leave the rice in the bowl under running water for several minutes until the water almost runs clear. Drain the rice in a colander and leave for 30 minutes.

Transfer the rice to a rice cooker or a saucepan with a well-fitting lid. Add the measured water and allow to stand for 15 minutes. If using a rice cooker, turn it on and the rice will cook automatically. If using a saucepan, ensure that the lid is tightly closed throughout the cooking process, bring rice to the boil over medium heat, then reduce to a low heat and cook until all the water is absorbed (15–20 minutes). Allow the cooked rice to stand for 15 minutes.

Make the vinegar mixture in a separate bowl, by combining the rice vinegar, sugar and salt and mixing well.

Transfer the rice into a *hangiri* (flat wooden vessel) or a large bowl. Pour in the vinegar mixture and work it through the rice using a wet wooden rice paddle. Gently mix the rice using the paddle's edge, taking care not to crush the grains.

Cool the rice with a hand fan (a magazine or piece of cardboard also does the job adequately), while mixing gently with the paddle in a slicing motion until the rice is at room temperature.

Do not refrigerate, as this dries out the *sushi* rice and causes the starch to break down.

Sweet Red Beans

Red beans are an important ingredient in Japanese desserts, where they are often made into a paste or served whole, as in the recipe for 'Mitsumame (Fruit and Japanese Jelly with Sweet Red Beans in Syrup)' on page 121. Red beans are high in protein and low in fat.

MAKES 1 QUANTITY OF COOKED SWEET RED BEANS

1 cup (220g/7oz) raw red beans, rinsed and soaked in water for 4–5 hours (optional)
2 tablespoons castor sugar
a pinch of salt

Place the beans in a pan, add water to cover the beans 3cm (1¼in) above. Bring to the boil rapidly, over a high heat, with the lid on. Add 1 cup of cold water and bring it back to the boil. This is a traditional step believed to soften the skin of the bean. Remove from heat and drain.

Return the beans to the pan again and add water to cover the beans with 3cm (1¼in) of water above. Bring rapidly to the boil with the lid on, then simmer for a couple of minutes. As before, add 1 cup of cold water, bring back to the boil, then remove from heat and drain.

For the third time, return the beans to the pan and add enough water to cover the beans to 3cm (1¼in) above. Bring to the boil over high heat, then lower heat and simmer for 50–60 minutes, until the beans become soft. If necessary, top up water to keep the beans covered.

Place a cotton cloth in a bowl, and tip in the red beans. Gently squeeze to extract excess water, taking care not to crush the beans. Transfer the beans to a pan and add the sugar and salt, stirring gently over a low heat until the sugar dissolves. Set aside to cool, then store chilled in the refrigerator until required.

Egg Mimosa

Egg Mimosa is widely used in modern Japanese cooking. It is useful for adding texture to a dish and binding ingredients together.

MAKES 1 QUANTITY (ABOUT 3 TABLESPOONS)

1 hard-boiled egg

Shell the egg, remove the yolk and discard the white. Using a wooden spoon, gently push the yolk through a sieve into a bowl, to make a light, moist powder. During this process, the mass of the ingredient increases greatly.

Preparation Techniques for Fish and Seafood

Three-piece Filleting Technique

1 whole salmon, 1.5–3 kg (3–6lb)

Most salmon is sold cleaned. But if the fish still has its guts, make a slit from the tail to the head along the belly with a sharp knife and open. Pull out and discard the insides and rinse the cavity under running water. Scale the fish using a *uroko-tori* (Japanese fish scaler) if possible, as it causes less damage to the fish.

Wipe the fish dry so that it is easier to work with. Position the fish flat on a board with the tail on the right hand side If you are right-handed, and hold the fish with your left hand. Reverse if you are left-handed. Insert the knife at the top of the fish head, just behind the head bone, with the blade angled slightly toward the fish head. Following the natural curve of the cheek, continue slicing in one smooth stroke behind the gills to the depth of the backbone, until you reach the underside of the fish. Holding the knife flat and the blade facing away from the fish head, insert the knife into the very top ridge of the of the fish head just behind the head bone (as pictured top left). In one swift movement, slice the knife diagonally through the fish with the knife kept flat along the back bone, allowing the knife to cut though the flesh of the belly edge too. Continue in a drawing motion until you reach the tail and the fillet is free. Set the fillet aside and turn the fish over, again placing the tail on the right hand side of the board. Repeat all steps as above, but when making the second cut (along the backbone), insert the knife point sideways at the underside edge rather than the top of the fish.

Place the fillets cut side up on the board. Holding the knife on a fairly flat angle, cut from the centre of the fillet to belly edge, removing lower belly parts (as pictured left, second from top).

Place the fillet on the board, skin side down. Run your finger along the fillet to check for bones. . Remove any bones with a pair of tweezers (as pictured bottom left).

Wipe the knife clean. Hold onto the tail end of a fillet with one hand (your left if you are right-handed), skin side down. Insert the knife at a slight angle just above the skin at the tail end, and move the knife along the skin about 5cm (2in) into the fillet. Holding the fish firmly, remove the knife. Gently pull the free flesh back just enough to hold the knife vertically above the skin you've just cut free from the fish. Make a 2cm (¾in) incision into the skin, cutting lengthwise about 2cm (¾in) from the tail edge. This will create a 'buttonhole' that runs parallel to the length of the fish. Insert your left thumb into the 'buttonhole' in order to prevent the slippery skin from moving. Hold the knife flat side facing up, and begin cutting from the tail end near the buttonhole, just above the skin. Keeping the knife held flat just above the skin, carefully slice towards the head end in one continuous movement to free the flesh from the skin. Repeat with the other fillet.

Sashimi Slicing Techniques

Sashimi *slicing techniques vary according to the type of fish. Here are the two main techniques:*
hiki-zukuri and sogi-zukuri. *For both, you will need a long fillet of fish that is 6cm (2½ in) wide*
and a clean, wet cloth. Filleting techniques are presented on the opposite page.

HIKI-ZUKURI

This is a basic *sashimi* technique to slice fish into pieces 2.5cm (1in) thick.

Place the fillet on a chopping board and hold onto the fillet with your left hand (reverse if
you are left-handed). With a *sashimi* (filleting) knife slice the fish into pieces 2.5cm (1in) wide.
After each cut, slide the piece along the cutting board about 10cm (4in) away from the fillet.
Arrange the pieces neatly in a layered row. Balance the layered pieces on the flat side of
the knife and transfer to serving dishes.

Wipe the knife clean with the cloth.

SOGI-ZUKURI

Sogi-zukuri is a technique for *sashimi* and *sushi* tops. This slice is thinner than *hikizukuri sashimi,*
so it creates a different sensation in the mouth.

Hold onto the thicker end of the fillet with your left hand (reverse if you are left-handed).
Insert the *sashimi* knife at a 45-degree angle into the fish and slide the knife towards the
·left to make a thin slice about 1cm (½ in) wide. Slice the remaining fillet into 1cm (½ in)
wide pieces.

CLEANING OF CALAMARI, SQUID AND CUTTLEFISH

Hold the calamari or squid tube in one hand and with the other hand pull out the tentacles.
The insides should come away with the tentacles. Cut off and discard the guts and ink sac.
Pull out the hard 'bone' inside the body and discard. Reserve the tentacles—they are edible.

Dry the calamari or squid with a cloth or paper towel. Holding the body with one hand, grasp
one flap and pull it away from the other. Remove the skin by carefully rubbing it away with
a cloth. Rinse and wipe dry.

Place the calamari or squid on the board, and cut lengthwise through the tube to open it.
Remove any dark parts inside. Turn over so that inside of the flesh is face down on the board.

Slice into thin julienne with a filleting knife or prepare for *nigiri-zushi* or cooking by making
shallow diagonal cuts at 1cm (½ in) intervals along the surface. (Do not cut through.)
Repeat with the opposite diagonal to create a crosshatch pattern.

PREPARATION TECHNIQUES FOR VEGETABLES

PREPARATION OF VEGETABLES FOR STEW

Pumpkins, turnips and carrots are fine examples of the kinds of vegetables that are suitable for Japanese stews. These vegetables hold their shape and texture throughout the cooking process, and look pleasing to the eye when served. Vegetables that flake after cooking, such as potatoes, are, therefore, not suitable.

SMALL VEGETABLES

This method works well for small vegetables that are best served whole, such as baby turnips, or very small satoimo.

Hold the vegetable in one hand. Using a small knife, peel by making one cut from the stem to the bottom. Continue working around the vegetable working from top to bottom, keeping the width of the cuts as uniform as possible, and aiming to have all cuts meeting neatly at the bottom, in imitation of the vegetable's natural, round shape.

LARGE VEGETABLES WITH PEEL

This method is useful for large, thick-skinned vegetables that need to be cut into small pieces before they can be served, such as pumpkin. Many varieties of pumpkin have distinctly different coloured skin and flesh. With a little work you can accentuate this contrast and make a great visual addition to your dishes.

Begin with an unpeeled piece of pumpkin measuring 5cm x 6cm (2in x 2½in) across the surface of the skin. Neatly make a cut 1cm (½in) away from the skin and slice off the flesh, leaving a piece of pumpkin 1cm (½in) thick with the skin still on. Place on a board with the skin facing up. With a small knife, trim the piece into a leaf shape as shown in the photo. Using the tip of the knife, draw a simple design on the surface of the skin, pressing hard enough to cut through the skin, but not into the flesh. Insert the knife below the skin and remove skin from within each shape outlined, leaving flesh showing through from beneath.

SHAPING WITH CUTTERS

This is the easiest way to create interesting shapes with vegetables. All you need are metal vegetable cutters; if they are unavailable, small cookie cutters can be substituted. Vegetables need to be chosen according to the size of the cutters.

Slice, but do not peel the vegetable. (The skin is cut off when you stamp out the shape with the cutter.) The thickness of the slices will depend on the type of vegetable you are cutting, but generally, between 3mm–5mm (⅛in–¼in) is ideal. Place the slices on a wooden board (to avoid damaging cutters on a hard surface) and push the cutter through each slice.

Garnishes

Japanese cooking uses many garnish ideas to enhance the beauty of the cooked dish. Many of these ideas come from nature, and may vary according to the season. Popular motifs include flowers, leaves, birds or insects.

Once a vegetable is sliced, the moisture content evaporates quite quickly, leaving the vegetable dry and the juice weak. Keep the sliced vegetables in cold water until ready to use to avoid loss of flavour and moisture.

Shredded Daikon

MAKES 1 QUANTITY (ABOUT 60g/2oz)

1 daikon
iced water

Peel the *daikon* and cut out a 10cm (4in) cylinder. Holding the *daikon* in one hand, place the edge of the knife vertically on the daikon and move the knife in a sawing motion to 'peel' a continuous sheet of *daikon* of uniform thickness. Make a sheet of up to 10cm (4in) long.

Roll up the *daikon* gently without breaking, and cut into thin julienne. Soak in iced water until ready to use.

Harangiri

Harangiri is an inedible leaf carved with a small knife. It is a popular garnish in traditional Japanese cooking. Inexperienced cooks who are less skillful at carving and 'turning' with a knife, could use small cutter shapes instead. Bamboo, camellia and aspidistra leaves are all suitable for harangiri.

Using the tip of a small knife, on each leaf lightly draw the outline of a smaller leaf inside. Cut through the leaf along this outline, being careful to leave the outside edge intact.

CUCUMBER FAN

The cucumber fan epitomises the classic simplicity of Japanese shapes. It is found in most stylish and traditional Japanese restaurants. Unlike harangiri, *this is an edible garnish.*

TO MAKE 4 FANS

1 large cucumber or 1 small winter melon

Using a small knife, cut the cucumber in half lengthways. Place the halved cucumber cut side down, leaving the skin intact. Cut both halves widthways into four 5cm x 7cm (2in x 2¾in) pieces. Remove the seeds in one neat cut, leaving 1cm (½in) flesh attached to the skin.

Using the tip of the knife, draw a fan shape over each skin. Trim, cutting cleanly to this outline. Using the knife tip, draw a design inside the fan, as shown in the photo, pressing lightly to cut through the surface of the skin but not into the flesh, leaving a border about 2mm wide around the edges. Insert the knife under each shape of the internal design and remove the skin in these areas to leave the white flesh showing from beneath, to form a pattern on the fan. Soak in water until ready for use.

CRANE

Like the cucumber fan, the crane is a beautiful, traditional and edible Japanese garnish.

TO MAKE 4 CRANES

1 large cucumber or 1 small winter melon

As for the cucumber fan above, use a small knife and cut the cucumber in half lengthways. Place the halved cucumber cut side down, leaving the skin intact. Cut both halves widthways into four 5cm x 7cm (2in x 2¾in) pieces. Remove the seeds in one neat cut, leaving 1cm (½in) flesh attached to the skin.

Using the tip of a knife, draw a crane outline on the skin, as shown in the picture. Trim carefully to this shape, leaving the silhouette of the crane. Using the knife tip, draw a design on the 'body' as shown in the picture, pressing lightly to cut through the surface of the skin, but not into the flesh. Leave a border of skin approximately 2mm wide around the edges. Insert the knife under each internal outline and carefully remove the skin from these areas, leaving the white flesh showing beneath, creating a pattern on the body. Soak in water until ready to use.

SAMPLE SET MENUS

SIMPLE MENU FOR BEGINNERS 1

Apéritif: Sake (page 22)

Entrée: Tuna and Salmon Sashimi (page 51)

Main Course: Miso soup with Tōfu and Shıtake (page 45), a bowl of steamed
rice and Diced Daikon with Kiwifruit Sauce (page 107)

Tea: Bancha or Sencha (page 127)

SIMPLE MENU FOR BEGINNERS 2

Apéritif: Matcha and Lemongrass Cocktail (page 19)

Entrée: Green Winter Melon and Fish Cake in Clear Soup (page 43)

Main Course: Chirashi-zushi (Scattered Sushi) (page 101) and Nanohana with
Yuzu and Shichimi Salad (page 111)

Tea: Bancha or Sencha (page 127)

FORMAL SUMMER MENU

Most of the dishes included on this menu can be pre-prepared and kept chilled until needed.

Apéritif: Grapefruit and Mandarine Sake (page 22)
Entrée: King Prawn Wrapped in Harusame (page 33)
Soup: Cold Green Pea Soup with Daikon Flower (page 41)
Sashimi: Combination Sashimi on Ice (page 49)
Stew: Diced Pork in Broth (page 63)
Grill: Grilled Garfish with Mushroom (page 69)
Yosemono: Green Tea Tōfu (page 77)
Sushi: Tazuna-zushi (Twisted Rope Sushi) (page 99)
Salad: Cold Pork with Plum Dressing and Daikon (page 109)
Dessert: Mitsumame (Fruit and Japanese Jelly with Sweet Red Beans) (page 121)
Tea: Mugicha (Cold Barley Tea) (page 127)

FORMAL WINTER MENU

Apéritif: Hot sake (page 23)
Entrée: Cheddar Cheese with Ume Paste and Nori (page 31)
Soup: Miso Soup with Pork Loin and Seasonal Vegetables (page 45)
Stew: Fuki-Yose Stew of Seasonal Vegetables (page 59)
Grill: Grilled Salmon with Roasted Rice (page 73)
Agemono: Satsuma-age (Deep-fried Fish Cakes) with Shītake (page 89)
Sushi: Nigiri-zushi (Hand-moulded Sushi) (page 92)
Salad: Tomato and Calamari Salad with Shiso-ume Purée (page 105)
Dessert: Nashi and Kiwifruit Bavarois (page 119)
Tea: Gyokuro (page 126)

GLOSSARY

AONORI flaked green *nori* (seaweed)

AZUKI red beans often used to make a sweet paste

BAINIKU paste made from the flesh of *umeboshi* (pickled plum)

BENISHŌGA red pickled ginger

CHA tea

DAIKON large white radish

DAIKON-OROSHI grated *daikon* served as a condiment

DASHI Japanese stock

DŌMYŌJI-KO steamed, then roasted or dried sticky rice

ENOKI cream-coloured mushrooms with long thin stems and tiny caps

GARI sliced pickled ginger in vinaigrette

GOMA black or white, roasted or unroasted sesame seeds

GOMA-SHIO salted sesame seeds

GOMA-DARE sesame seed paste

HANGIRI sushi bowl

HARUSAME Japanese vermicelli

HIBACHI charcoal burner

HIKI-ZUKURI sashimi slicing techinique

HŌUCHŌ Japanese knife

HŌBA leaf of the plant *Ficus lyrata*, used for wrapping food

KAIWARE (*Kaiware-daikon*) giant white radish sprout

KAKI Japanese sweet persimmon

KANPYŌ dried gourd strips

KANTEN jelly-like substance made from red algae, available in stick or powder form

KATAKURIKO potato-starch substitute

KATSUO-BUSHI shaved dried bonito, used for dashi

KINOME young leaves of sanshō (prickly ash tree)

KOMBU (KONBU) edible dried black kelp commonly used to make dashi

KOME Japanese short-grain rice

KOMEZU Japanese rice vinegar

KURI chestnuts

KUZU potato starch

MAGURO tuna

MATCHA green tea powder

MIDORI Japanese liqueur made from honeydew melon

MIMOSA sieved egg yolk

MIRIN sweet cooking rice wine

MISO soybean paste

MITSUBA member of the parsley family, used as a garnish

MIZUDAKI a hot-pot dish

MOMEN-DŌFU firm beancurd

MYŌGA Japanese ginger

NANOHANA canola (rape) shoots and flowers

NASHI Japanese pear

NIGIRI-ZUSHI hand-moulded sushi

NORI dried seaweed sheet

OCHOKO small sake cup

RENKON fleshy root of the lotus (*Nelumbo lutea*)

SAIBASHI pair of long chopsticks used for cooking

SAKE Japanese wine made by brewing rice

SANSHŌ prickly ash tree leaves

SASHIMI sliced raw fish

SATOIMO Japanese potato with a waxy, glutinous texture and high sugar content

SHICHIMI a mixture of seven hot spices

SHĪTAKE shītake mushrooms (available dried or fresh)

SHIMEJI Japanese variety of mushroom with a fat cap and stem

SHISO leaves and buds of the perilla or beefsteak plant, used in salads and as a garnish

SHISO-UME *ume-boshi* (pickled plum) and *shiso* combined to make a paste

SHUNGIKU spring chrysanthemum leaves, used as a vegetable

SOBA buckwheat noodles

SOGI-ZUKURI technique for *sashimi* and *nigiri-zushi* tops

SUDARE rectangular bamboo mat used for rolling *sushi*

SURIBACHI bowl used for grinding spices

SŌMEN thin Japanese noodles

TAKENOKO young bamboo shoots

TAKUAN pickled Japanese radish

TEMPURA deep-fried dishes

TENTSUYU *tempura* dipping sauce

TERIYAKI grilled (broiled) meat or beancurd, basted with sweet soy sauce to give the finished dish a glossy texture

TOBIKKO flying fish roe

TŌFU beancurd: may be firm (*momen-dōfu*), or soft (*kinugoshi-dōfu*)

TOKKURI *sake* serving bottle

TSUMA shredded daikon, used with sashimi, as a condiment

UGO salted seaweed

UMAMI the scale of deliciousness that measures the taste of glutamate

UME-BOSHI pickled plums

UNAGI Japanese (black-fin) eel

UROKO-TORI fish scaler

WASABI Japanese green horseradish

YUKARI dried, salted and flaked purple (red) basil (*shiso*)

YUZU Japanese citrus zest obtained from a variety similar to lemonade fruit

YUZU MISO sweet *miso* paste with Japanese citrus zest

INDEX

DRY WEIGHTS		LIQUID WEIGHTS			TEMPERATURES			
10g	½oz	1 metric teaspoon	5ml		Celsius	Fahrenheit		
30g	1oz	1 metric tablespoon	20ml		100°	210°	Very slow	
50g	1¾oz	1 UK/US teaspoon	5ml		125°	240°	Very slow	
60g	2oz	1 UK/US tablespoon	15ml		150°	300°	Slow	Gas mark 2
85–90g	3oz	¼ metric cup	60ml	2fl oz	180°	350°	Moderate	Gas mark 4
100g	3½oz	½ metric cup	125ml	4fl oz	200°	400°	Moderately hot	Gas mark 6
120–125g	4oz (¼ lb)	1 metric cup	250ml	8fl oz	220°	450°	Hot	Gas mark 7
150–155g	5oz	4 metric cups	1 litre (2 pints)	1¾ pints	250°	475°	Very hot	Gas mark 9
185g	6oz	1 UK pint	20fl oz					
200g	7oz	1 US pint	16 fl oz					
250g	8oz							
500g	16oz (1lb)							
750g	24oz (1½ lb)							
1kg	32oz (2lb)							